International Fall Festivals

Projects and Patterns for Holiday Gifts, Greetings, Ornaments, Decorations, and Classroom Displays

Written and illustrated by
Marilynn G. Barr

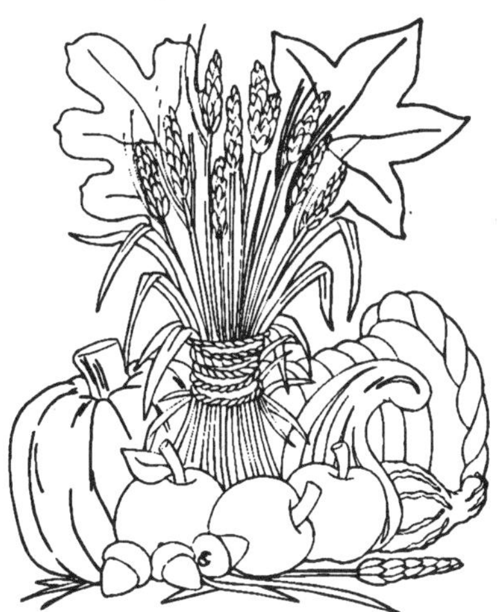

Cover by Marilynn G. Barr

ISBN No. 0-86653-818-6

Printing No. 9876

Good Apple
A Division of Frank Schaffer Publications
23740 Hawthorne Boulevard
Torrance, CA 90505-5927

Table of Contents

Table of Contents

Introduction

Fall, also known as autumn, is a time of change. The autumnal equinox occurs in the month of September when the sun moves slowly to the south. Weather grows colder, leaves on trees change colors, and seasonal plants begin to die. People prepare for the long winter months, and farmers work long hours to harvest crops grown through the spring and summer months. It is a time of thanksgiving for a good harvest and sharing with friends and family. Animals prepare for winter as well. Birds fly south, and other animals, like squirrels, groundhogs, bears, and certain mice, gather food before their long winter sleep.

Autumn occurs during the months of September, October, and November north of the equator in the Northern Hemisphere and during the months of March, April, and May south of the equator in the Southern Hemisphere.

Harvest festivals are traditionally held during the fall. Many harvest celebrations originated in European countries. Some festivals included religious ceremonies of thanksgiving for a fruitful harvest season, while others were held in honor of specific historical events and people.

Introduce your students to multicultural fall holidays from around the world with the hands-on projects, activities, and background information featured in *International Fall Festivals*. Invite students to share what they learn with friends and relatives as they travel to different lands to celebrate traditional and contemporary fall holidays.

International Fall Festivals features interesting facts on the origins of traditions and customs; hands-on cut-and-paste activities for gifts, greetings, decorations, bulletin board displays; and more. Projects include corn husk crafts, leaf collages, mobiles, and miniature flag patterns for an international fall festival celebration. Use the patterns as they appear to decorate your classroom. Attach student-made flags to crepe paper or ribbon streamers. Also included at the end of each section are take-home notes. Use the notes to request craft supplies or family volunteers to share a fall festival experience with your class. Eliminate the text on each note to use for student writing exercises or display borders.

Fall festivals are great occasions for families to work, sing, dance, and share meals together. And regardless of the month of the year, autumn will continue to be a time of celebration and thanksgiving around the world.

This book is dedicated to Baby Bell, B-Dot,
and all the children from whom I receive my inspiration.

AFRICA

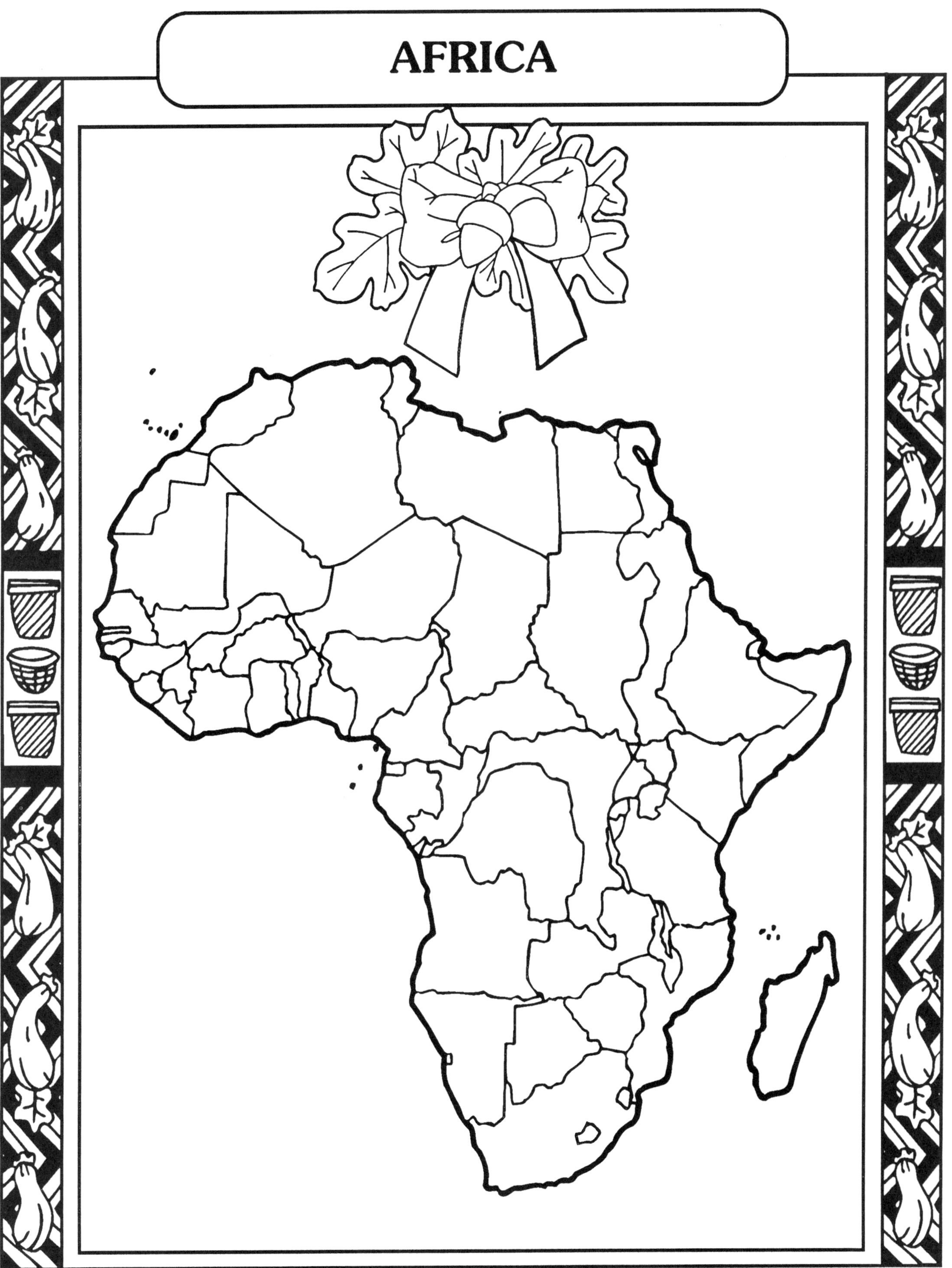

HOLIDAY TRADITIONS & LEGENDS
Africa

Many holidays are celebrated during the fall in Africa. Families gather to participate in religious ceremonies, share traditional meals, sing songs, dance, and tell stories during these special events.

Angola

During the harvest months, children celebrate the *Feast of Okambondondo*. Children of the same age celebrate the feast together. They bring cornmeal, corn, beans, meat, and fish to one location to prepare food to be eaten in the middle of the night. They play games and tell stories before going to bed, the boys in one place and the girls in the kitchen. Then late into the night the girls prepare the food and go to wake the boys to share the feast. After the meal they all go singing into town. The leftover meal is then taken home to their parents.

Cameroon

The people of Cameroon celebrate the Christian holiday *Evamelunga,* Thanksgiving Day, in September. Bright flowers and palms decorate churches. Families dress in their best clothes and sing on their way to Thanksgiving religious services.

Ethiopia

Ethiopians celebrate the new year in September. On the eve of the new year, girls gather wildflowers to make tiny bouquets. Early the next morning they gather to sing and visit homes wishing each family they visit a good new year. The bouquets are used as "thank-you" gifts for presents received from each household. The boys make bundles of branches on New Year's Eve to use as torches to light their way as they go from house to house singing new year songs. Boys also receive gifts (coins) from each household.

Anthrosht, Mother's Day, is celebrated in the fall after the rainy season. Children collect the necessary ingredients to prepare a traditional Mother's Day meal early in the day for mothers to serve later in the evening. The children sing songs in honor of special people in their families during the two- to three-day celebration.

ORNAMENTS & DECORATIONS • ETHIOPIA

New Year Bouquets

Invite students to make miniature flower bouquets to decorate windows, doors, and desks for an Ethiopian New Year's celebration. Provide each student with the leaf pattern, template, and materials listed below.

Materials:
- 2 plastic straws
- 1 letter envelope (new or used)
- crayons or markers
- glue
- scissors

1. Seal the envelope and cut straws in half.
2. Cut out the flower template.
3. Place the template over one corner and trace the scalloped edge onto your envelope.
4. Cut the corner of the envelope as indicated on the template.
5. Color the flower with crayons or markers.
6. Open your paper flower. Insert one straw half through the hole in the corner and secure with tape.
7. Repeat steps 3-6 for each remaining corner of your envelope.
8. Color and cut out the leaf pattern.
9. Apply glue where indicated.
10. Gather the flowers and wrap the leaf pattern around the straws.

Anthrosht Greeting Cards

Reproduce the patterns on construction paper and provide the materials listed below for each student to make a take-home Anthrosht (Mother's Day) greeting card that stands on its own.

Materials:

- magazine for cutout pictures
- scissors
- glue
- crayons or markers

1. Color and cut out the patterns along the bold lines.
2. Draw or glue cutout pictures in the blank space on pattern A.
3. Fold and apply glue to the tab on pattern B.
4. Attach pattern B to pattern A as indicated and allow to dry.
5. Write a message under the flap.

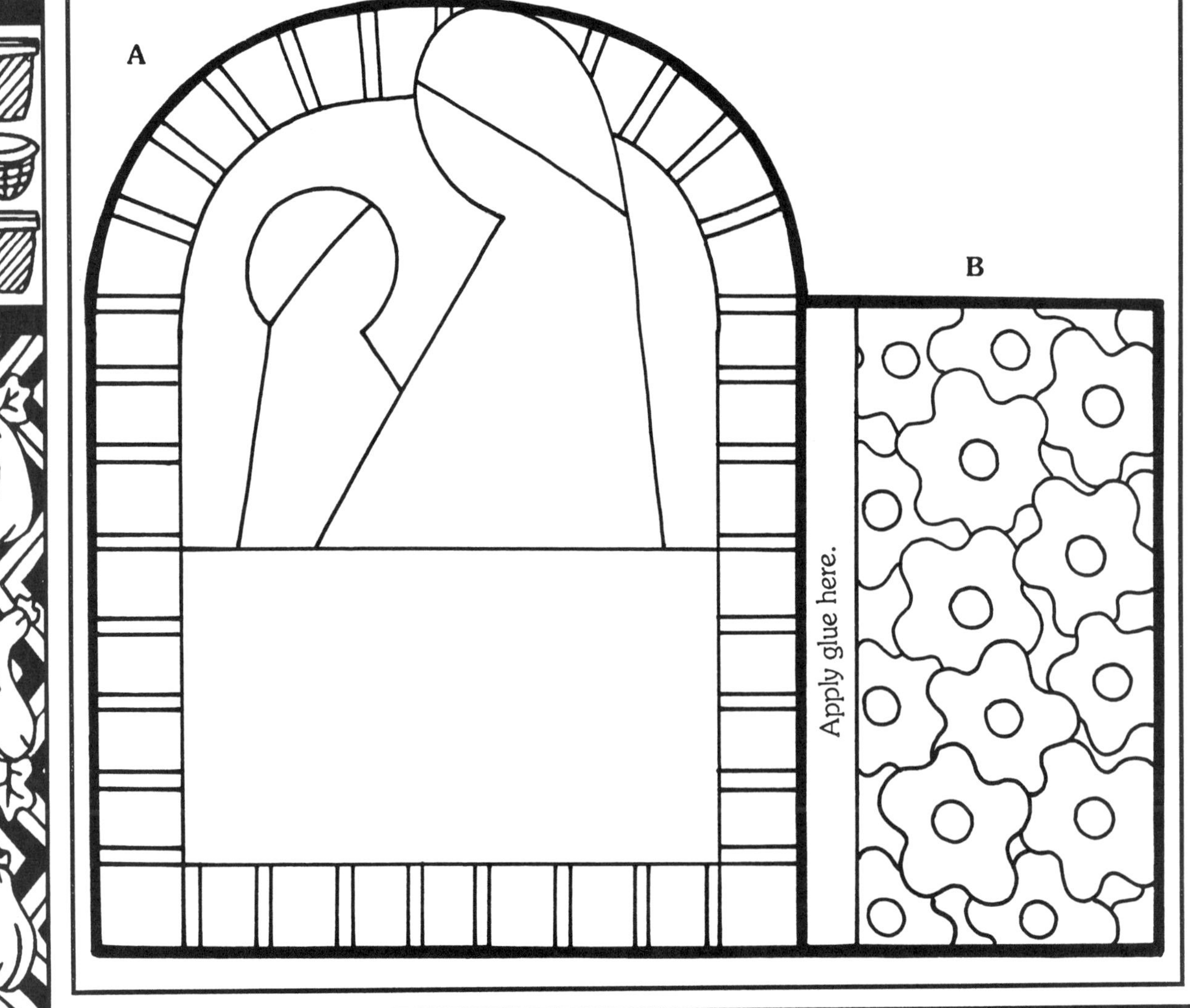

Africa

Ghana

Odiwera is one of several harvest festivals held in Ghana. It is also known as the "first fruit festival." There are a variety of stories that tell of the origins of this yam festival. One ancient legend tells of a hunter who found an unfamiliar fruit in the wilderness. When he returned to his home he discovered that an animal was eating the yam and reported it to the chief. The chief ate the yam and waited to see if this "new fruit" would harm him. After several days passed, the chief remained unharmed and the yam was declared good to eat.

In keeping with the events of the legend of the discovery of the "new fruit," it is forbidden to eat yams from the new harvest for a number of days, until a series of traditional events take place. Once these events take place, yam festivals are held; the yams are declared ready to eat and are offered to each household.

Libya

Both schools and businesses close to celebrate the national holiday honoring the prophet Muhammed's birthday. The day is filled with contests and parties concluding with fireworks displays in the evening.

Children make *khumaisa* (koo-my-SAH), hand-like decorations, which are displayed everywhere. The khumaisa can be made of wood or cardboard. Decorations also include glass bells, colored pinecones, and silver paper cut-outs.

Kingdom of Swaziland

The people of Swaziland celebrate Independence Day on September 6. They gained their freedom from Great Britain in 1968.

Mauritania

Mauritanians celebrate their independence on November 28. They gained their independence from France in 1960.

Peoples Republic of Benin

Also governed by France and originally named Dahomey, the Peoples Republic of Benin celebrates its national holiday on November 30.

A Yam Festival

Decorate your classroom with these student-made Yam Festival windowpanes. Solicit parent volunteers to help students complete this project. Prepare a table with the materials listed below and provide each student with patterns and two yellow construction paper frames.

Materials:

- 2 sheets of clear ConTact™ paper (5" x 5" or 12.7 x 12.7 cm)
- scissors
- stapler
- yarn
- a hole punch
- cellophane tape

3.

Clear ConTact™ paper

5.

6.

1. Color and cut out the patterns.
2. Peel the backing from one sheet of ConTact™ paper.
3. Carefully position the patterns in the center of the ConTact™ paper.
4. Peel the backing from the remaining sheet of ConTact™ paper.
5. Carefully place it over the patterns.
6. Position the window on one of the frame patterns and secure it with cellophane tape.
7. Align the remaining frame over the window and staple all sides together.
8. Punch two holes at the top of your windowpane.
9. Lace and tie a length of yarn through the holes for hanging.

A Yam Festival

ORNAMENTS & DECORATIONS • GHANA

Odiwera Clay Art

Encourage children to paint creative scenes of the "First Fruit Festival" to celebrate the discovery of yams in Ghana. Prepare a table covered with newspapers and provide students with the materials listed below.

Materials:
- 8" x 8" (20 x 20 cm) corrugated board
- pencils
- brushes
- water to rinse brushes
- 10" x 10" (25 x 25 cm) oaktag or poster board
- a hole punch
- yarn
- colored clay slip

Clay Slip Recipe:
- 1 part clay
- 3 parts water
- Add food coloring to achieve the desired color.

1. Use a pencil to draw a scene showing the discovery of the yam on a sheet of corrugated board.
2. Dip your brush in colored clay slip to color your picture. Allow each color to dry.
3. Apply glue to the back of your finished picture.
4. Attach your picture to a sheet of oaktag or poster board.
5. Punch two holes at the top of your picture.
6. Lace and tie a length of yarn through each hole.

Khumaisa Decorations

Provide sheets of dark colored construction paper, chalk, and the materials listed below for students to make decorations for a Libyan holiday celebration.

Materials:
- dark colored construction paper
- chalk
- glue
- glitter
- scissors
- yarn

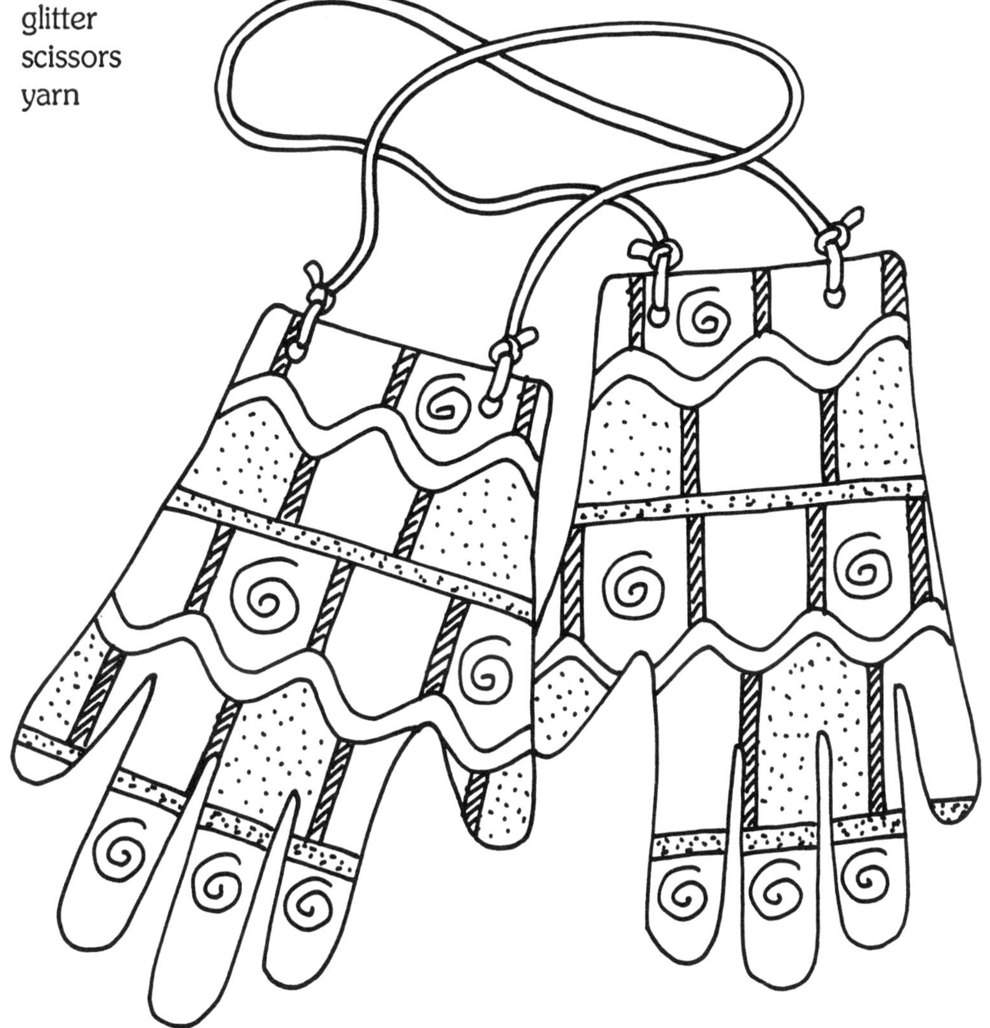

1. Trace your hands onto a sheet of construction paper.
2. Color and decorate your hands with chalk, glue, and glitter.
3. Punch two holes at the top of each hand.
4. Lace and tie a length of yarn through each hole for hanging.

Africa

Republic of Kenya

Kenyatta Day is a public holiday celebrated in October honoring Jomo Kenyatta, the first president of the independent Republic of Kenya.

We Celebrate Our Independence

A number of African countries celebrate national holidays or their independence from foreign rule during the fall months of September, October, and November. Invite students to help decorate a bulletin board celebrating African holidays entitled We Celebrate Our Independence.

Display a festive colored background on your bulletin board. Enlarge, color, and cut out the map of Africa on page 1 and attach it to the center of the board. Provide students with the African flag patterns found on pages 162-187, the fireworks pattern below, crayons, and scissors to color and cut out for a festive bulletin board display.

Use the take-home note on page 11 to ask parents to send cupcakes for students to enjoy when the bulletin board is finished. Provide students with additional fireworks patterns to make cupcake toppers. Have students color, cut out, and attach fireworks to a toothpick with tape.

A TAKE-HOME NOTE FROM
AFRICA

____
Date

Dear ______________________________,

We are ____
____.

Please ____

Thank you!

____
Teacher

ANTARCTICA

Antarctica

Antarctica is virtually uninhabitable. However, plankton, a mass of tiny animal and plant life (and an important part of the ocean food chain), grows in Antarctic waters. A few creatures such as birds, fish, penguins, seals, and whales can also be found along the coasts which serve as breeding grounds.

Legends of Antarctica

Invite your students to create a legend about Antarctica that occurs during the autumnal equinox on September 23. It's the time of the year when the sun crosses the equator moving slowly to the south.

Give each student a list of creatures that could be included in their stories, for example, the Abominable Snowman, the elusive unicorn, Bigfoot, or a polar dragon, to name a few. Then reproduce and provide students with patterns on pages 14-16 to make displays and greetings to support their legends.

A Flag for Antarctica

Reproduce the pattern on page 21 or provide a 4" x 6" (10.16 x 15.24 cm) sheet of paper for students to design flags for Antarctica. Provide students with a variety of craft supplies: geometric construction paper shapes or templates, crayons, markers, and glitter. Use the flags to decorate student legends. Glue each student's legend to a sheet of colored construction paper or poster board. Using a hole punch, punch two holes along the upper right edge of the poster board. Thread the finished flag through the holes as shown and secure with tape. Display student work on a bulletin board entitled "Legends of Antarctica."

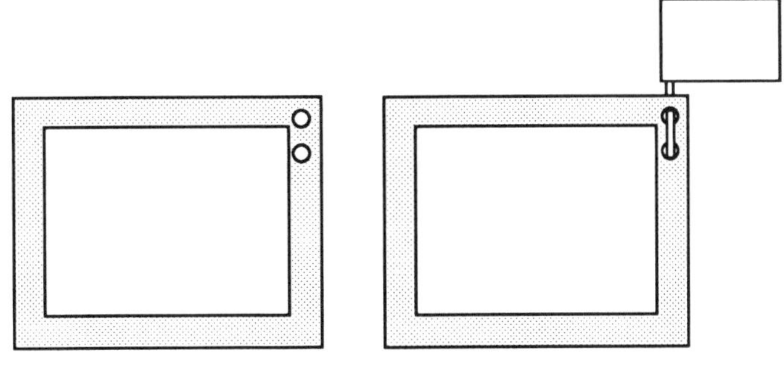

Abominable Snowman

Unicorn

Polar Dragon

Creatures of Antarctica

Invite student participation in preparing a bulletin board showing creatures that are occasionally found near Antarctica's coast. Cover your board with light blue bulletin board paper. Have students draw snowflakes using light blue markers or crayons on 3" x 12" (7.62 x 30.48 cm) strips of white construction paper. Enlarge the map of Antarctica on page 12 and mount it in the center of the board. Reproduce the ice rafts below on white paper and position around the map. Use a blue marker to write the title on white poster board.

Reproduce and provide the patterns on pages 18-20 for students to color, cut out, and display on the bulletin board.

Penguins

Seals

Whales

A Flag for Antarctica

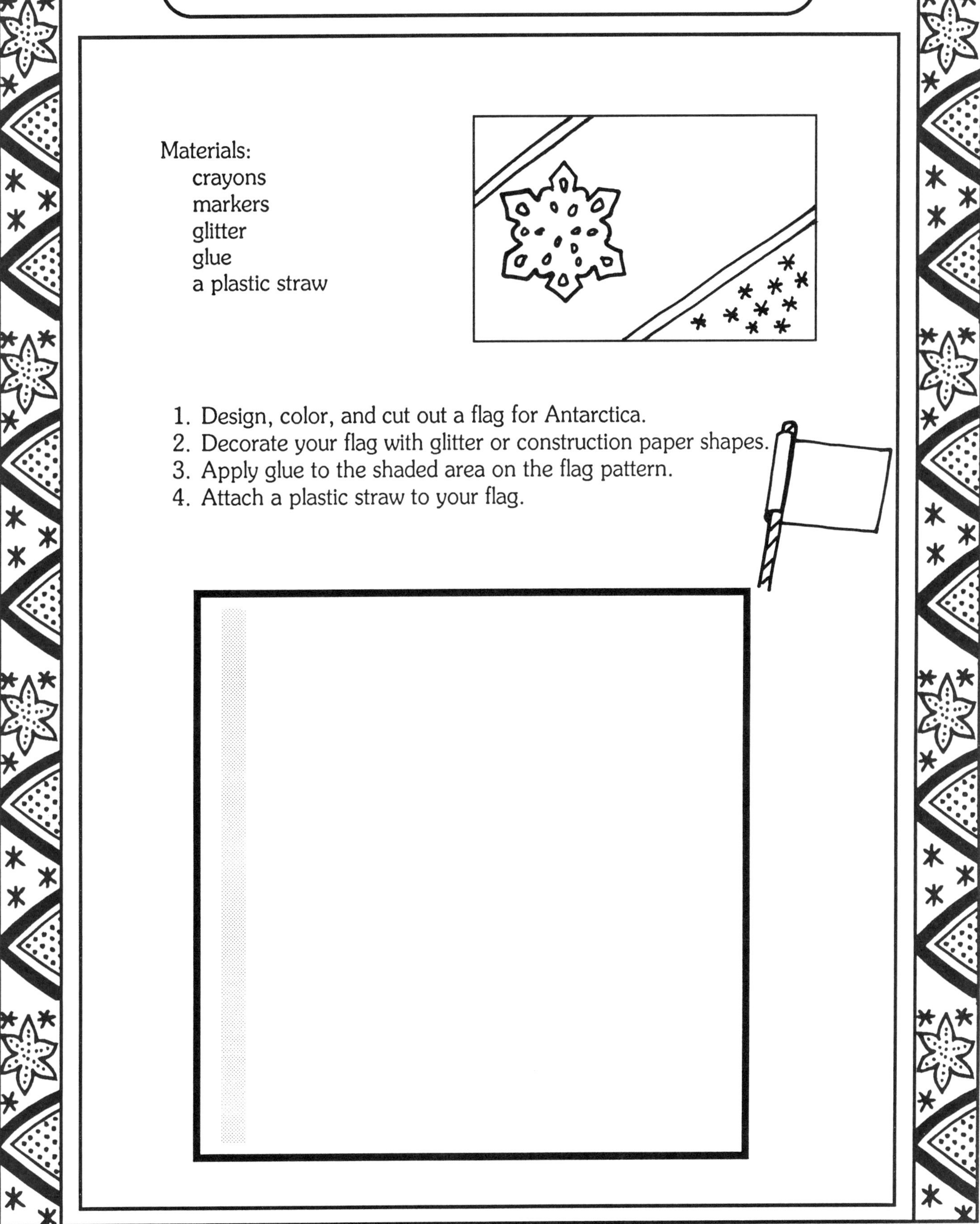

Materials:
- crayons
- markers
- glitter
- glue
- a plastic straw

1. Design, color, and cut out a flag for Antarctica.
2. Decorate your flag with glitter or construction paper shapes.
3. Apply glue to the shaded area on the flag pattern.
4. Attach a plastic straw to your flag.

A TAKE-HOME NOTE FROM
ANTARCTICA

Date

Dear ,

We are .

Please

Thank you!

Teacher

ASIA

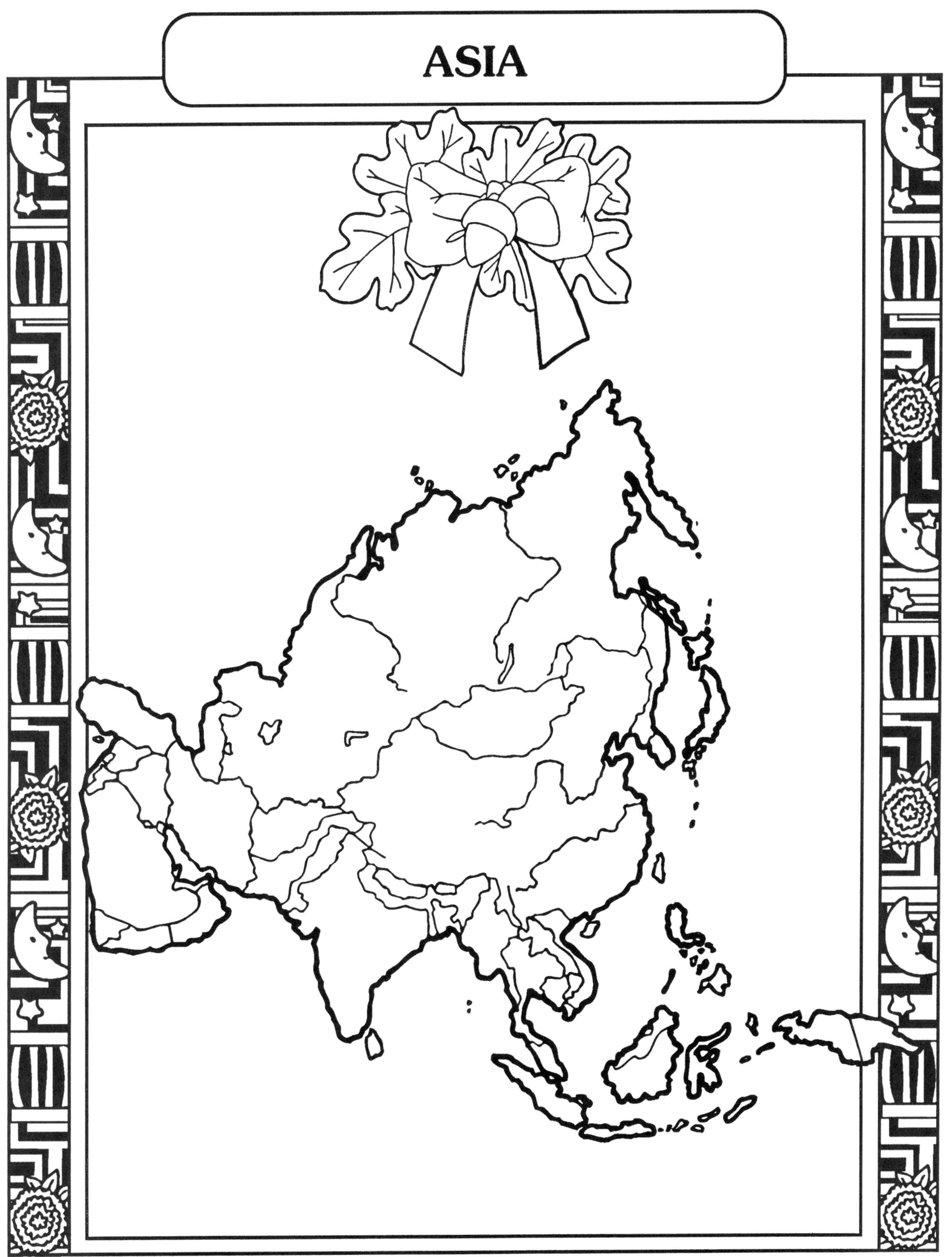

Asia

Burma

In October the people of Burma celebrate the end of Lent, a religious season of fasting, with a *Festival of Lights*. This celebration occurs at the end of the rainy season. Homes are decorated with lights, fireworks light the skies, and tiny rafts float along the rivers.

Cambodia

Cambodians celebrate the end of the rice harvest and the advent of the rainy season. It is the happiest time of the year. A feast is shared among the villagers. The meal includes a variety of foods: pork, melons, bamboo sprouts, and roast lizard. All the while gong music fills the air until sunset.

Iran

Flowing sounds from the *shofar* bring the promise of a good New Year on *Rosh Hashanah*. During this two-day holiday observance no food or drink is taken until after the religious services. On Rosh Hashanah eve families share meals which include fruits and vegetables that symbolize a good year. For example, apples in sugar were served to symbolize a sweet year.

Israel

Simhat Torah, celebrated in September-October, marks the completed annual cycle of readings from the Jewish bible, the Torah.

Is'ru Chag follows Shimat Torah and marks the beginning of the new cycle of readings. This event is celebrated with the sounds of music.

Festival of Lights Raft

Use the take-home note on page 59 asking for parent volunteers and clean Styrofoam™ trays to complete this project.

Use a sharp pencil or other tool to punch holes as indicated below. Provide students with the pattern and materials below.

Materials:

- Styrofoam™ tray
- construction paper sail
- crayons or markers
- a hole punch
- a plastic straw
- yarn

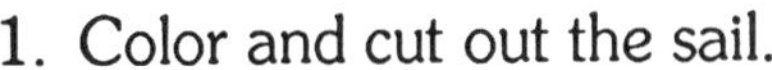

1. Color and cut out the sail.
2. Punch a hole at each dot and thread a plastic straw through the holes as shown.
3. Cut a length of yarn and lace it through the holes in your tray as shown in the diagram below. Attach additional lengths of yarn as needed.
4. Tape loose ends of yarn to the bottom of the tray.
5. Punch a hole in the center of the tray.
6. Insert the sail in the hole and secure with a ring of glue as shown. Allow to dry before moving.

2.

6.

Glue.

3.

Miniature Rice Harvest Gong

Provide the materials listed below for students to complete this project.

Materials:
- margarine tub lid
- yarn (7" or 17.78 cm)
- crayons or markers
- scissors
- glue
- a hole punch
- 2 cotton swabs

1. Color and cut out the pattern.
2. Glue the pattern to the top of a margarine tub lid.
3. Punch two holes at the top of the lid and one at the bottom.
4. Lace and tie a length of yarn through each of the two holes at the top of the lid.
5. Cut off one end of each cotton swab.
6. Cross the swabs as shown and secure with a length of yarn to the bottom of the gong as shown.

HOLIDAY COOKING • IRAN

Sweet Apple Delights

Serve baked apple treats filled with brown sugar and raisins to celebrate Rosh Hashanah. Solicit parent volunteers to help prepare the treats.

Ingredients: (8 servings)

- 4 large apples
- 1 t. lemon juice
- cinnamon
- 1/2 cup raisins
- 1/2 cup brown sugar
- 1 T. melted butter

Cut apples in half. Use a melon spoon to scoop a well in the center of each apple half. Cut the scooped apple into small pieces.

Prepare a mixture of 1/2 cup brown sugar, 1 teaspoon lemon juice, 1/2 cup raisins, and the cut apple. Fill each apple half with the mixture.

Place each apple half in a miniature pie tin and bake at 350°F (176°C) up to 30 minutes or until tender (not mushy).

Allow to cool and sprinkle cinnamon over each apple before serving.

Japan

Chrysanthemum Day

Chrysanthemum Day is a quiet day dedicated to the viewing of elaborate floral displays. Families gather to share songs and picnics of boiled rice and chestnuts and chrysanthemum cakes under the trees. During *Choyo*, the Chrysanthemum Festival, they quietly view booth after booth of floral displays.

Jugoya are traditional, larger-than-life floral figures decorated almost entirely with tiny chrysanthemums. The head, hands, and feet are made of other materials. The flowers are secured to a kind of lattice structure fashioned from bamboo or wire. The background is made of tiny flowers and painted wooden objects.

Because these elaborate figures and scenes have become too expensive, they are rarely seen in Japan today.

Freeing the Insects

The Japanese participate in an ancient custom during the fall. Many families catch insects and keep them in tiny bamboo cages throughout the summer months to enjoy the sounds they make in the evenings. At the end of summer, people gather to participate in the ceremony of "freeing the insects." The ceremony takes place in public parks and places of worship. Once the insects are free, the people enjoy hearing their chirps of freedom.

Jugoya Collage

Reproduce the patterns on pages 29-30 for students to make colorful collages for a festive Chrysanthemum Day bulletin board display. Provide students with glue, cotton balls, spray bottles filled with diluted food coloring, and oaktag or cardboard.

Have students cut out the patterns. Instruct them to glue the doll pattern onto the background. Then have them glue the assembled scene to a sheet of oaktag or cardboard.

Show how to glue cotton balls, filling one section at a time. Then spray the cotton balls (chrysanthemums) with food coloring. Continue gluing and spraying until the entire pattern is covered.

Jugoya Doll

Jugoya Background

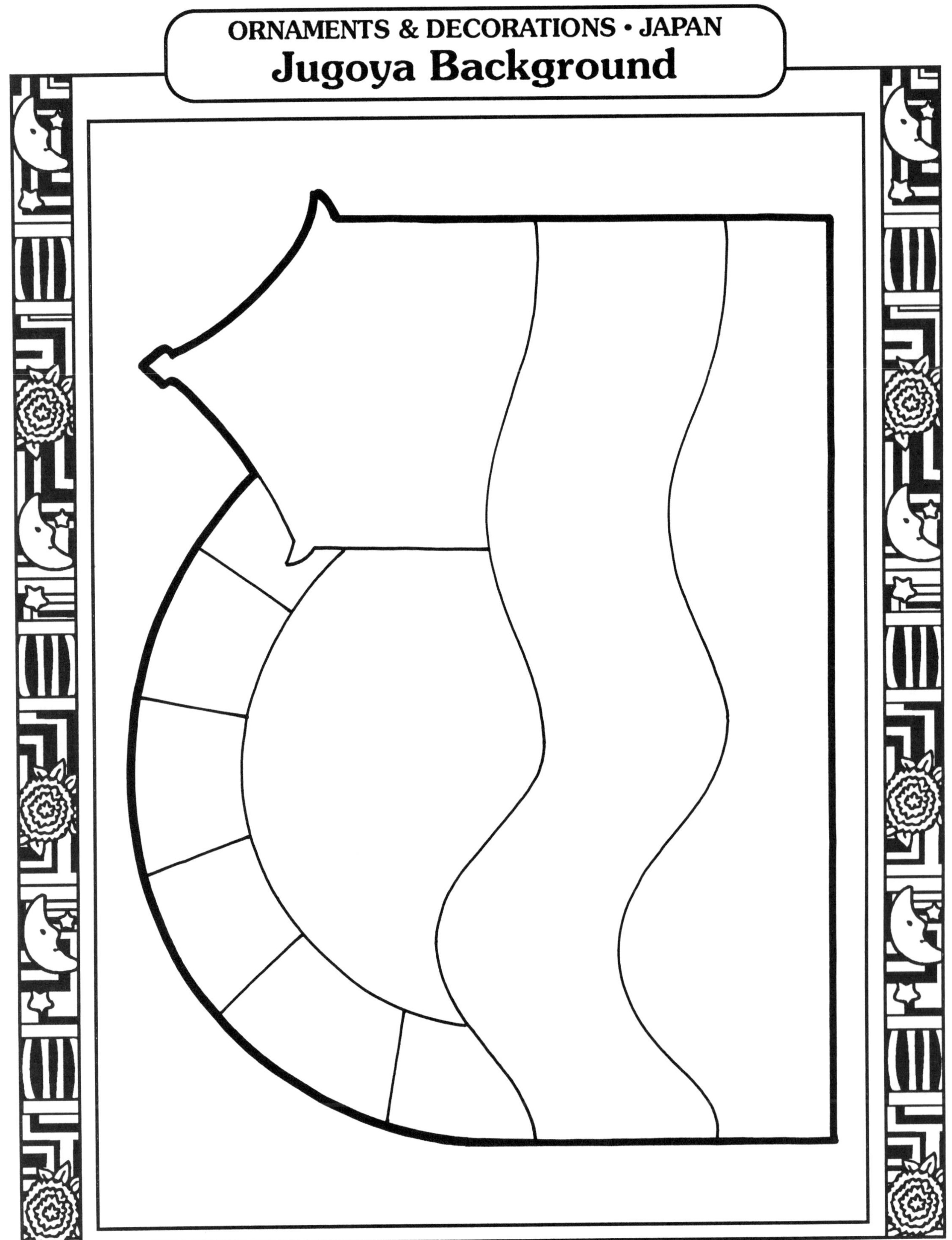

Chrysanthemum Fair

Chrysanthemum Fair

Transform your entire classroom into a chrysanthemum flower fair. Provide students with 4" (10.16 cm) colored tissue paper circles, a set of the flower patterns (below), crayons or markers, a hole punch, plastic straws, and cellophane tape.

Have students color, cut out, and punch a hole in the center of each flower pattern. Show how to fold, twist, then fluff the tissue paper circle to make a flower (diagram A). Insert the tissue flower in the pattern and secure it with tape. Attach a plastic straw to the back of the flower. Display finished flowers around your classroom.

For colorful garlands to decorate your classroom, reproduce the flower patterns on colored construction paper, punch holes on opposite sides, and lace ribbon or yarn through the holes.

Chrysanthemum Day Greetings

Provide each child with a 5" x 8" (12.7 x 20.32 cm) sheet of colored construction paper, crayons, scissors, glue, and cotton balls.

Have children fold construction paper in half to form a 4" x 5" (10.16 x 12.7 cm) greeting card. Then have them glue their flower patterns to the front of the card. Show how to glue cotton balls in the center of the pattern. Help students think of greetings to write inside their cards.

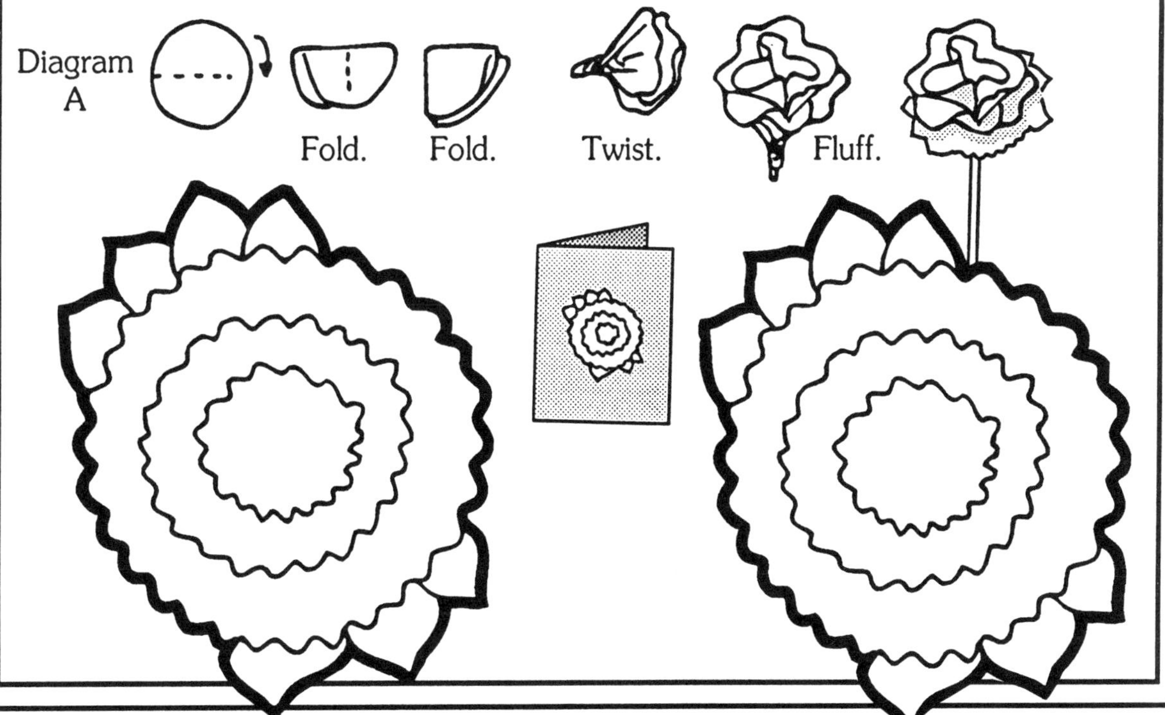

Freeing the Insects

Freeing the Crickets

Create a Freeing-the-Insects bulletin board display with these student-made cricket cages. As students complete their projects, encourage them to mimic cricket sounds as they mount their cages with open doors to free their crickets on the bulletin board.

Provide students with the patterns on pages 32-33, a sheet of colored construction paper, crayons or markers, scissors, and glue.

1. Color and cut out the cricket and cage patterns.
2. Carefully cut open the door.
3. Glue the cricket in the center of the sheet of construction paper.
4. Open the door on the cage and position it over the cricket making sure the cricket shows through the door.
5. Apply glue to the back of the cage along the edges and attach to the construction paper.
6. Write your cricket's name at the top of the construction paper.

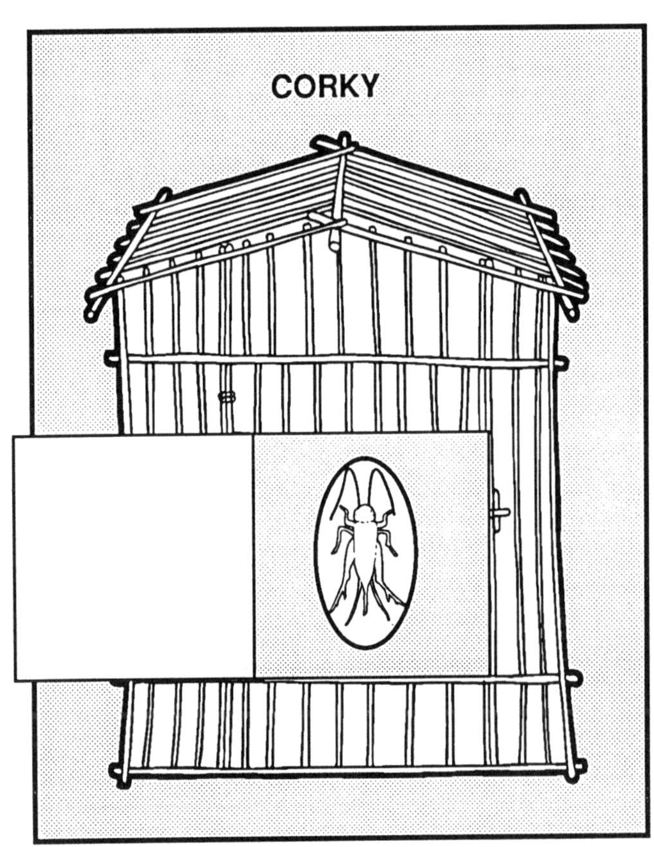

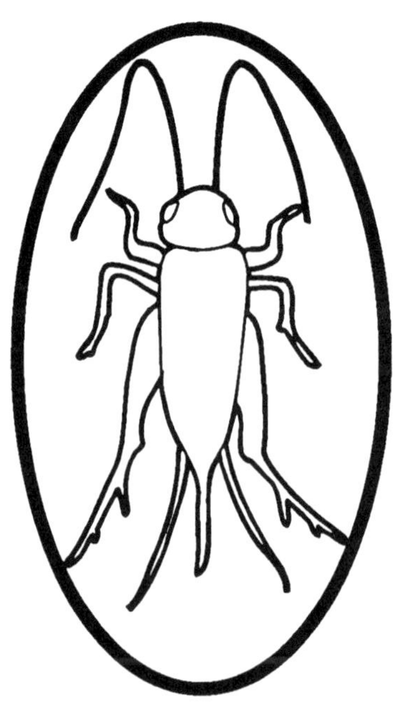

Freeing the Insects

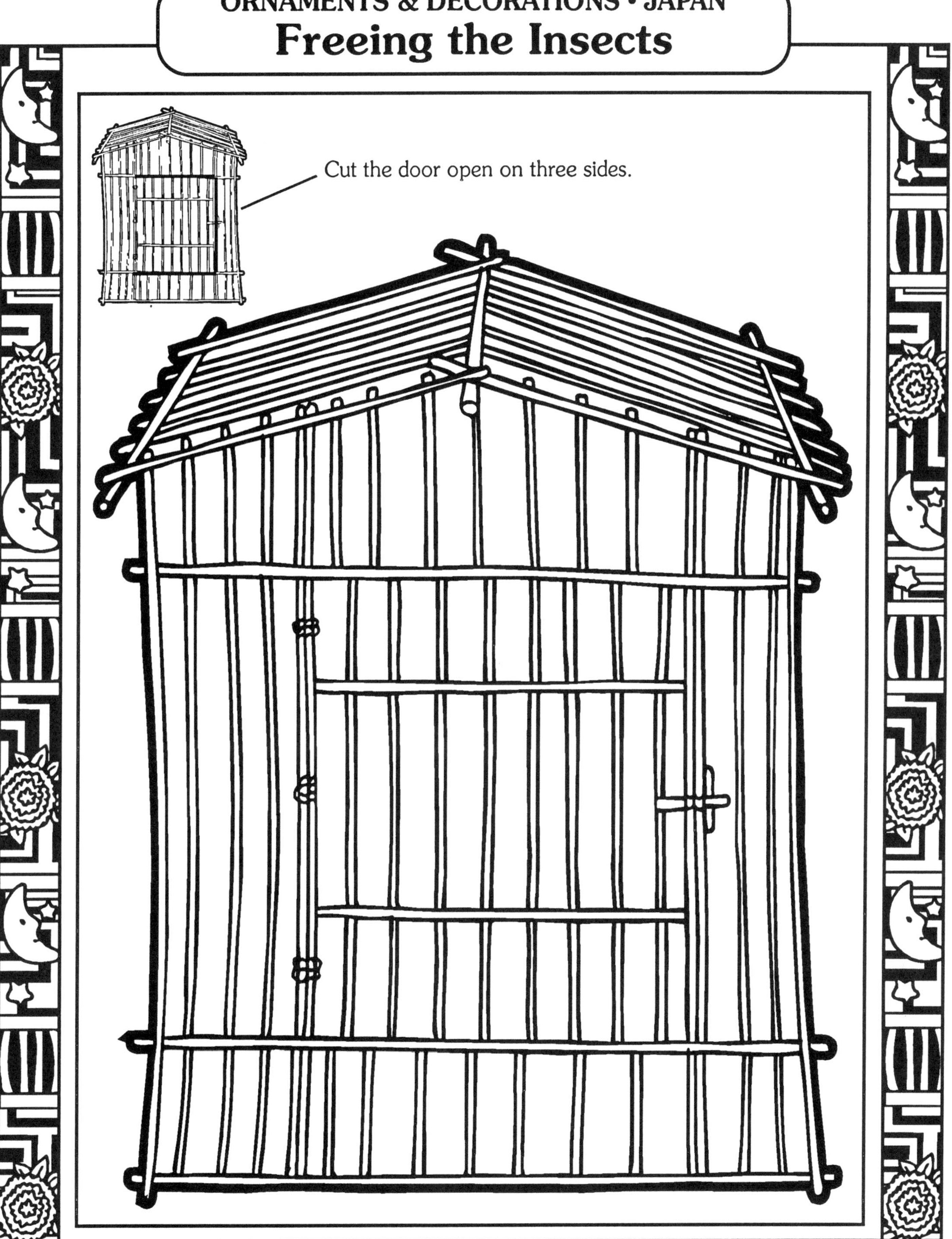

Japan

Keiro no Hi

Keiro no Hi (Respect for the Elderly Day) is a national Japanese holiday which originally included parties in honor of the elderly.

Although today parties are seldom held, persons over the age of seventy are presented with gifts of handmade clothing articles and charms (small objects believed to have magical powers).

Mega Kenka Matsuri

Mega Kenka Matsuri, a Roughhouse Festival, is held in October. Persons compete to show their ability to balance *palanquins*, covered chairs on poles carried on the shoulders of more than one person.

New Taste Festival

The *New Taste Festival* is a Japanese harvest festival and national holiday which occurs in the month of November to give thanks for the rice harvest.

Shichi-go-san

The festival of *Shichi-go-san* is celebrated in November. This is a special day for all three-year-olds, five-year-old boys, and seven-year-old girls. On this day, the children dress in their best clothes to receive special approval during a religious ceremony. At the ceremony each child receives "thousand-year candy," pink candy in long sacks. The candy is given for good luck and a long life.

In the past boys changed their hair styles and trousers in a ceremony known as the "Hakamagi." In the "obi-toki" ceremony, girls put on a sash (obi) like their mothers and big sisters.

GIFTS & GREETINGS • JAPAN

Keiro no Hi Pendants

Grandparents will enjoy receiving these student-made pendants celebrating *Keiro no Hi*, the Japanese holiday in honor of the elderly. Provide students with the patterns below, crayons or markers, scissors, a length of yarn, and a hole punch. Encourage children to draw pictures in the blank pendants or provide magazines for students to cut out pictures to glue to the center of their pendants.

HOLIDAY TREATS • JAPAN

Thousand-Year Candy

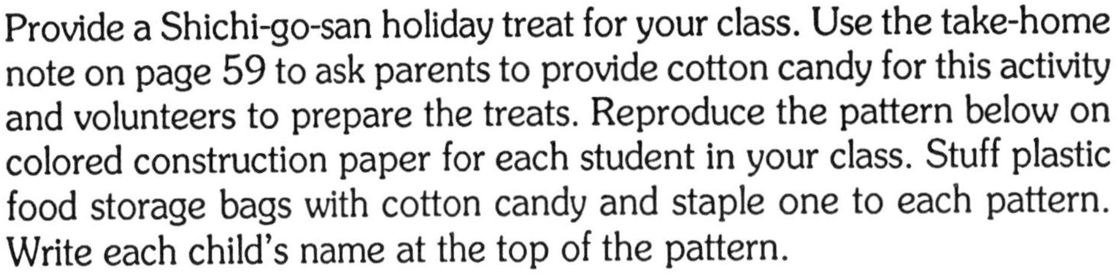

Provide a Shichi-go-san holiday treat for your class. Use the take-home note on page 59 to ask parents to provide cotton candy for this activity and volunteers to prepare the treats. Reproduce the pattern below on colored construction paper for each student in your class. Stuff plastic food storage bags with cotton candy and staple one to each pattern. Write each child's name at the top of the pattern.

Shichi-go-san Puppet

Provide each child with a girl or boy Shichi-go-san puppet pattern from pages 37 and 38, a Popsicle™ stick, crayons or markers, scissors, and glue. When students complete their dolls, display them on the bulletin board with their thousand-year candy.

1. Color and cut out the doll pattern.
2. Fold the pattern along the dotted line.
3. Apply glue to the inside of the pattern and place a Popsicle™ stick in the center of the bottom edge.
4. Write your name on the back of the puppet.

ORNAMENTS & DECORATIONS • JAPAN
Shichi-go-san Puppet

Provide each child with a girl or boy Shichi-go-san puppet pattern from pages 37 and 38, a Popsicle™ stick, crayons or markers, scissors, and glue. When students complete their dolls, display them on the bulletin board with their thousand-year candy.

1. Color and cut out the doll pattern.
2. Fold the pattern along the dotted line.
3. Apply glue to the inside of the pattern and place a Popsicle™ stick in the center of the bottom edge.
4. Write your name on the back of the puppet.

Asia

Korea

On October 5 a festival is held in Korea in honor of King Seong who invented the Korean alphabet. The festival is called *Han'gul*. During the three-day festival a variety of ceremonies are held. Also writing contests are held in schools.

Philippines

On Halloween, children gather to sing songs as they go from house to house, collecting "alms" (money). Later they huddle in the night to hear traditional Halloween tales.

Thailand

Chulalongkorn Day is celebrated in honor of the King Chulalongkorn, who ruled from the late 1800s to the early twentieth century. He carefully changed Thailand's image to one of a modern nation and, most importantly, abolished slavery. Ceremonies of honor are held in Bangkok and flowers are displayed at the foot of the king's statue.

The *Elephant Round-up at Surin* takes place in November. Trains from Bangkok bring elephants for performances, demonstrations, races and a tug-of-war between men and elephants.

ORNAMENTS & DECORATIONS • KOREA
A Han'gul Writing Notebook

Reproduce several sheets of the manuscript pages below and one cover (page 41) for each student in your class to make a writing practice notebook. Display notebooks during your fall open house for families to view.

1. Color and cut out the cover and manuscript pages.
2. Fold the cover along the dotted line.
3. Insert the manuscript pages and staple along the fold to make a notebook.
4. Practice your writing skills in your Han'gul Notebook.

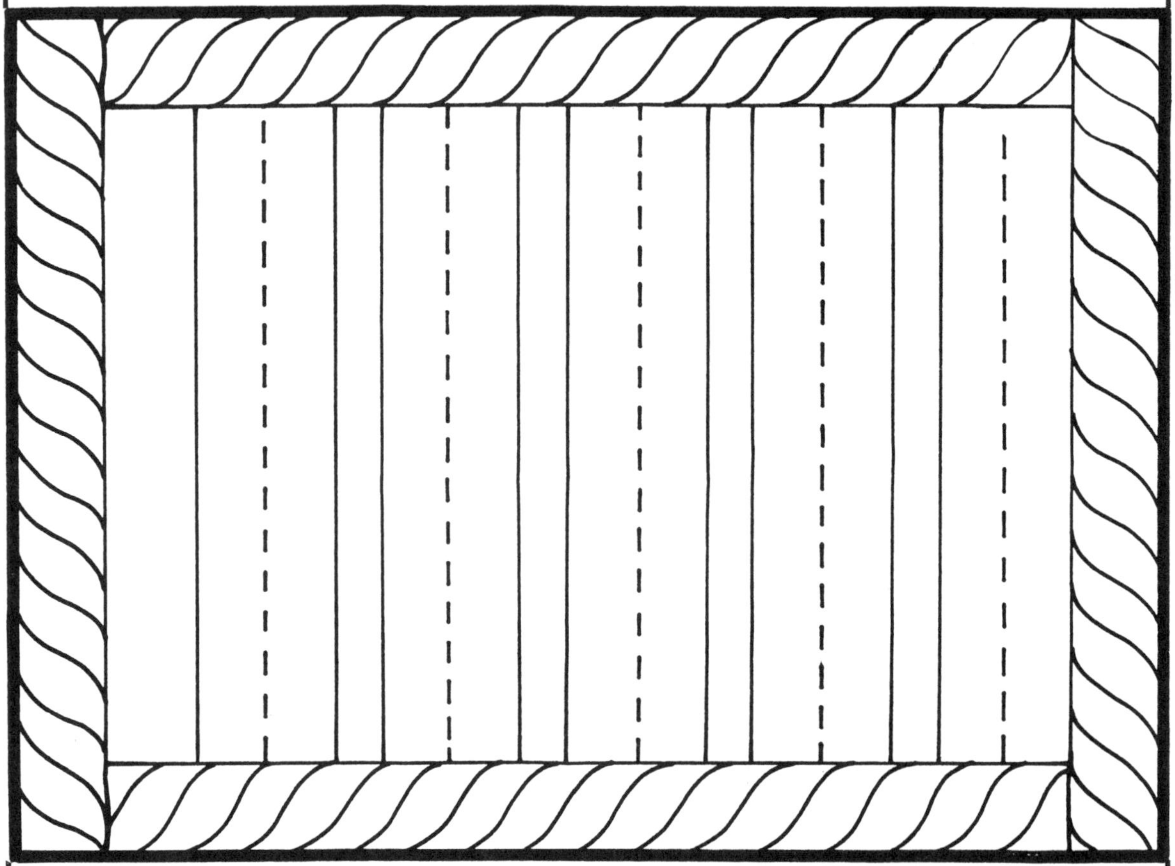

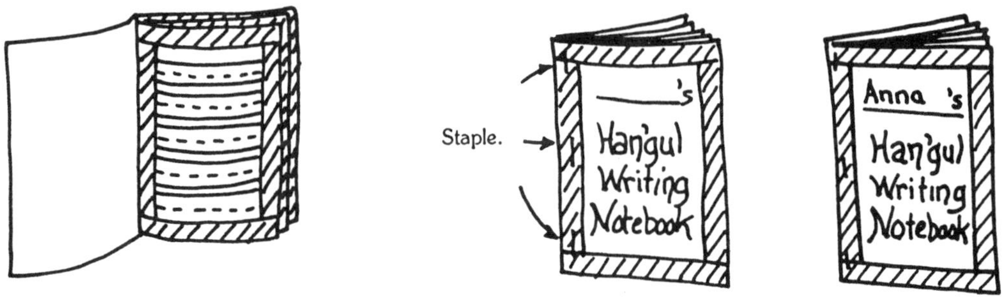

Staple.

's
Han'gul
Writing
Notebook

Anna 's
Han'gul
Writing
Notebook

A Han'gul Writing Notebook

Elephant Tug-of-War

Your students will enjoy creating this Elephant Tug-of-War bulletin board when they team up for a skills practice competition.

Divide your class into two teams. Reproduce the patterns on pages 43-44, elephants for one team, paper dolls for the other. Have each student color, cut out, and write his or her name on the pattern.

Cover your bulletin board with bright yellow paper and orange borders. Attach a length of yarn across the width of the board.

Instruct children to mount elephants on the left side and paper dolls on the right. When a student answers a question correctly, have him or her attach the pattern to the yarn across the board as shown. The team with the most patterns attached to the board wins.

Elephant Tug-of-War

Elephant Tug-of-War

HOLIDAY TRADITIONS & LEGENDS
Asia

Samoa

On *White Sunday*, Samoans honor their children. The children perform religious plays which they have rehearsed for weeks. And families share special meals with their children at the end of the day.

The children dress in white with flower wreaths on their heads. The day begins with a parade of children singing and carrying banners while walking to church where parents are seated and waiting. In turn, children present short dramas based on biblical stories throughout the morning.

Traditionally adults eat their meals before the children. However, on White Sunday the children eat first and as much as they want. Meals consist of pork, fruits such as bananas and coconuts, and pastries.

Syria

Syrians celebrate a special religious festival on Holy Cross Day in September. During the *Feast of the Crucifix,* which coincides with the grape harvest, families harvest, box, and carry grapes to an assigned location. They dip the grapes into a solution containing olive oil. Then the grapes are spread out and allowed to dry. At the end of the day families gather to dance and share a traditional feast.

A Bright White Open House

Greet parents at fall open house with pictures of your students in their Bright White attire in honor of Samoa's White Sunday celebration. Display photographs on white flower-shaped construction paper patterns. Mount on a bulletin board entitled "Dressed in Our Bright Whites."

Solicit parent volunteers to help students assemble their costumes using the patterns on pages 46-47 and take photographs. Have children recite poetry or read from a favorite book during the photography session to entertain students waiting on the sidelines.

For elaborate costumes, reproduce five additional three-dimensional flower patterns on page 47 for each student to attach to collars and headbands. Attach three flowers to the front of the headbands and two to each lower corner of the collar.

A Bright White Headband

Reproduce and provide each child with the patterns on pages 46-47 and a 4" (10.16 cm) white construction paper circle. Prepare a table with brass fasteners, a hole punch, scissors, and cellophane tape for students to assemble their Bright White costumes.

Headband

1. Cut out the patterns.
2. Tape the headband strips together to fit around your head.

Headband Strips

A Bright White Corsage

Boutonniere/Corsage

1. Cut out the flower patterns.
2. Punch a hole in the center of each flower pattern and a 4" (10.16 cm) circle.
3. Fold each petal along the dotted line.
4. Thread a brass fastener through the hole in each flower pattern, beginning with the smallest flower.
5. Glue the flower to a white construction paper circle.

A Bright White Collar

Provide students with a sheet of white construction paper, scissors, a hole punch, and yarn to make bright white collars. Have each student cut a semicircle to fit around his or her neck as shown above. Show how to use a hole punch to decorate the edges. Punch a hole on each side of the neck opening Tie a length of yarn through each hole.

Grape Harvest Festival

Transform your classroom into a grape arbor to celebrate Syria's grape harvest season. Provide students with grape patterns, purple crayons or markers, scissors, green pipe cleaners, and green yarn. Show students how to twist and attach pipe cleaner twirls around the stem. For a three-dimensional effect, provide purple pom-poms for students to glue on their patterns. Have each student write his or her name on the back. Hang the finished grapes from green crepe paper streamers, ribbon, or yarn draped around the classroom or bulletin board.

Taiwan

Double-yang, also known as Double Ninth, or *Teng-ko Choeh* (climbing up on high) in Taiwanese, is celebrated on the ninth day of the ninth lunar month in China. People go for a walk or enjoy picnics on hilltops.

One legend tells of a magician named Fei Ch'ang-fang and a man named Huan Ch'ing. Under the advice of Fei Ch'ang-fang, Huan Ch'ing took his family to the top of a high mountain to avoid a foreseen danger. When he returned to his home he found that he was wise to follow Fei's advice.

A festival based on similar legends is held in Hong Kong during October called the *Chung Yeung Festival.*

Confucius's Birthday in Taiwan

Confucius's birthday, a national holiday, is also celebrated as Teacher's Day in September. Confucius was a great teacher. The key to his way of thinking was based on kindness to others and goodness. He also valued good manners and the importance of self-improvement.

ORNAMENTS & DECORATIONS • TAIWAN

Double-Ninth 3-D Collage

Enlarge the patterns below for each student in your class. Provide students with crayons or markers, scissors, glue, and 1" (2.54 cm) lengths of green yarn to complete this project.

1. Color and cut out the patterns.
2. Fold the patterns along the dotted lines.
3. Apply glue to the bold lines and attach 1" (2.54 cm) lengths of green yarn.

4. Apply glue to the tabs where indicated and assemble the hill.
5. Apply glue to the tabs on the paper doll pattern and attach to the top of the hill as shown.

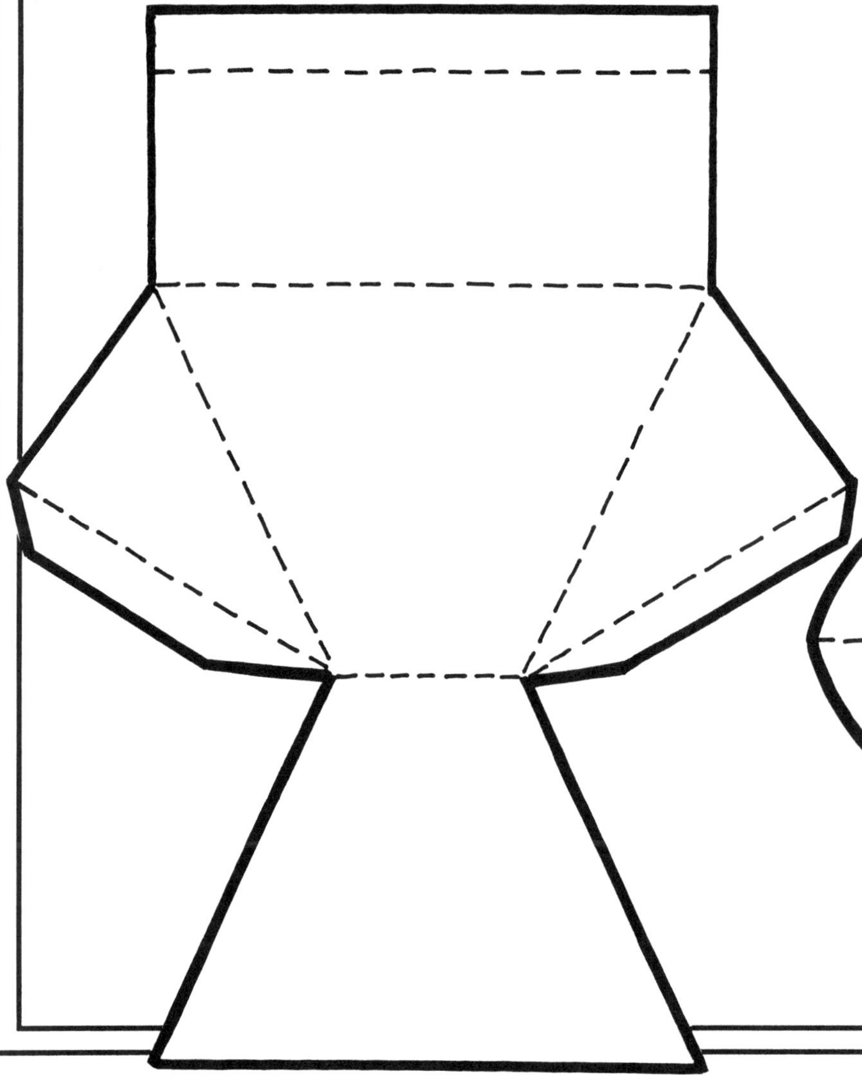

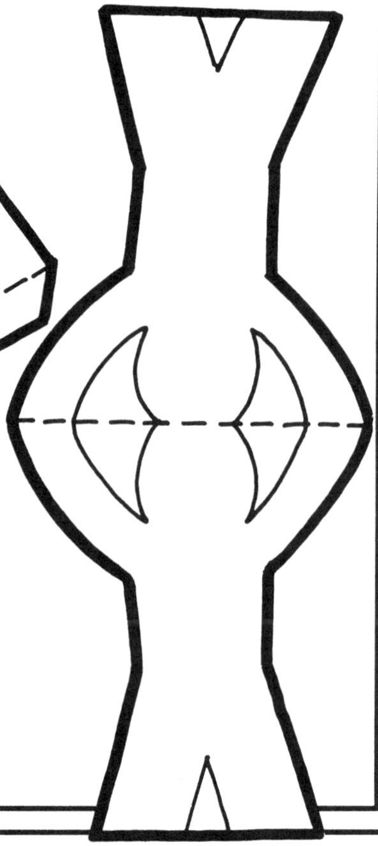

Great Teacher Greetings

Reproduce the pattern below and provide crayons or markers, yarn, scissors, and glue for each student to complete this project.

Ask students to write a message to a favorite teacher in the space provided. Mount finished greetings on colored construction paper. Trim around the pattern leaving a 1" (2.54 cm) border. Punch a hole at the top. Then lace and tie a length of yarn through the hole for hanging.

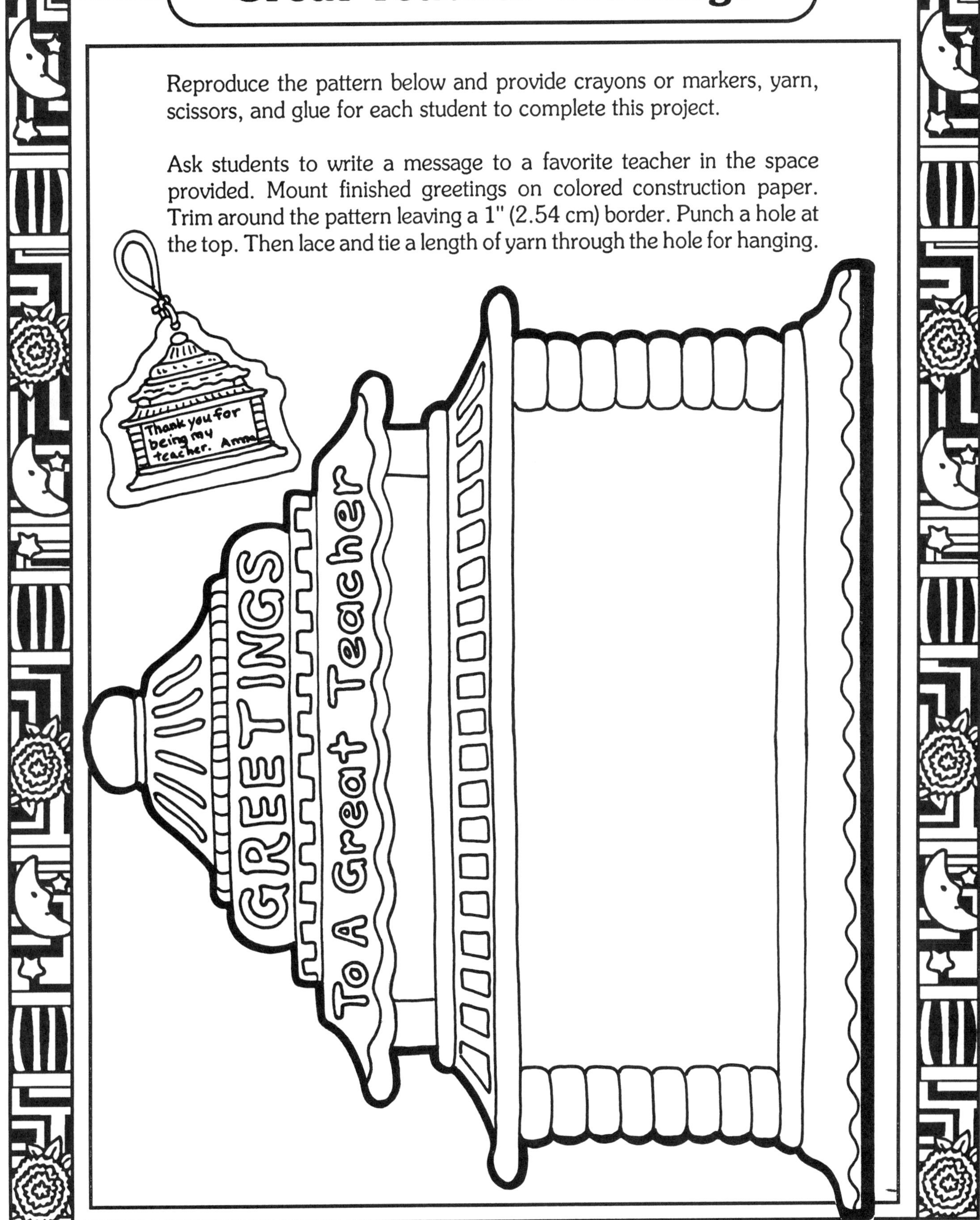

Vietnam

Tet-Trung-Thu

Tet-Trung-Thu is the biggest children's festival celebrated in September-October in Vietnam. It occurs on the fifteenth day of the eighth lunar month when the moon is full. Children enjoy moon cakes filled with a variety of ingredients such as raisins, watermelon seeds, sugar, and peanuts. Moon cakes are often sold in decorative boxes.

Legend tells the story of an ancient ruler who took his bride to a beautiful lake where he composed and read a poem to her by the light of the moon.

The children make boat, dragon, unicorn, and fish lanterns to light their way during the nighttime festivities. The lanterns are lit and the children parade through the streets on an imaginary journey to the moon, and the sounds of drums and cymbals fill the air.

Use the patterns on pages 54-58 and glow-in-the-dark paint to prepare for a moon walk to celebrate Tet-Trung-Thu with your class. Draw the shades and turn off the lights. Then watch your students beam as they watch their creations glow in the dark while they parade around the classroom.

HOLIDAY COOKING • VIETNAM

Moon Sandwiches

Your students will enjoy making Moon Sandwiches to celebrate Tet-Trung-Thu, Vietnam's biggest children's festival. Use the take-home note on page 59 to solicit parent volunteers to help students prepare these treats.

Prepare a table with peanut butter, raisins, and utensils. Provide each student with a paper plate and yellow stars to make a plate for his or her moon sandwich.

1. Cut out the stars.
2. Glue the stars around the border of your paper plate.
3. Wash your hands. Then spread peanut butter on a slice of bread.
4. Place a second slice of bread on top of the peanut butter.
5. Cut the sandwich into a circle to resemble a full moon.
6. Use raisins to add features to your moon sandwich.
7. Put your moon sandwich among the stars on your plate.

Moon Walk Lanterns

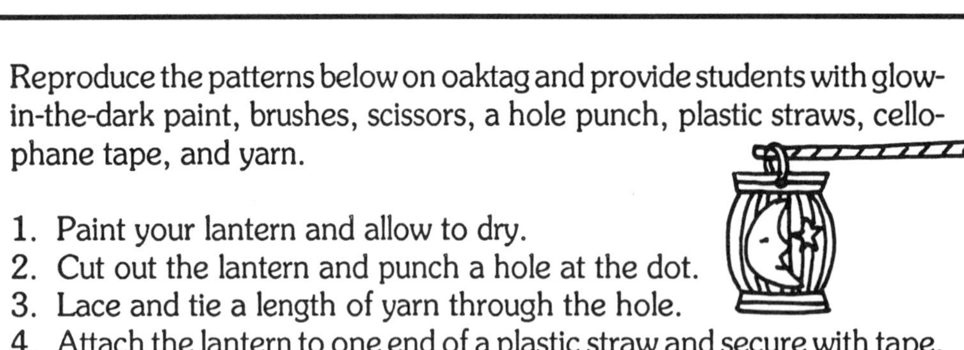

Reproduce the patterns below on oaktag and provide students with glow-in-the-dark paint, brushes, scissors, a hole punch, plastic straws, cellophane tape, and yarn.

1. Paint your lantern and allow to dry.
2. Cut out the lantern and punch a hole at the dot.
3. Lace and tie a length of yarn through the hole.
4. Attach the lantern to one end of a plastic straw and secure with tape.

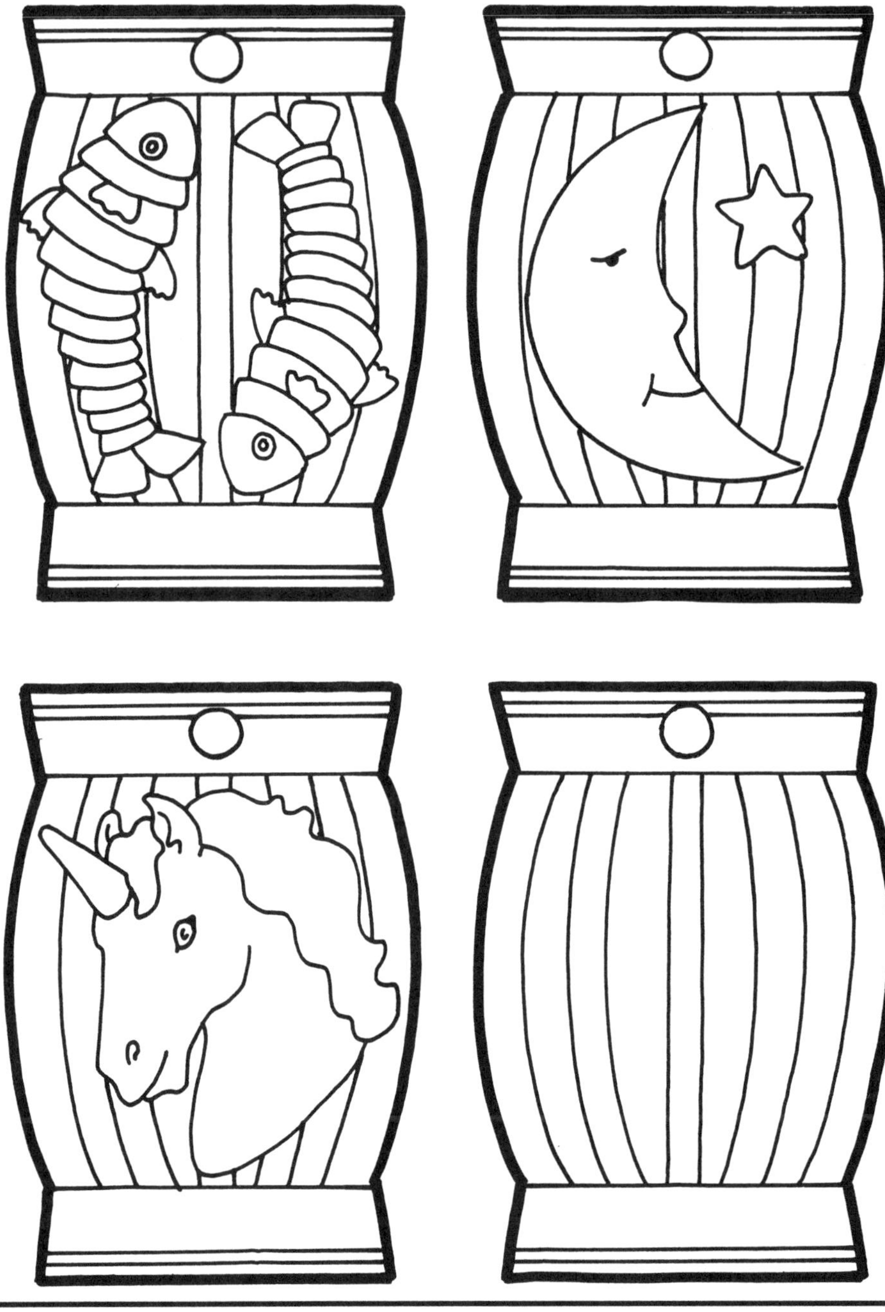

Moon Walk Cymbals

Use the take-home note on page 59 to ask parents to send four new or used aluminum pie tins to school with their children. Reproduce and provide each child with four oaktag cymbal covers, two paint stirrers, and glow-in-the-dark paint to make Moon Walk Cymbals.

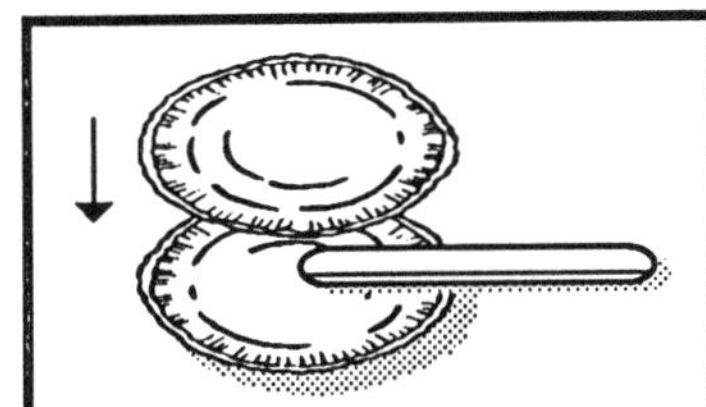

1. Paint the cymbal covers and allow to dry.
2. Cut out each cover and glue each one to the bottom of a pie tin.
3. Apply glue to one end of a paint stirrer and assemble the pie tins as shown above.
4. With supervision, staple through the pie tin to secure the paint stirrer.
5. Repeat steps 3 and 4 to make a second cymbal.
6. Bang your cymbals together during your Moon Walk parade.

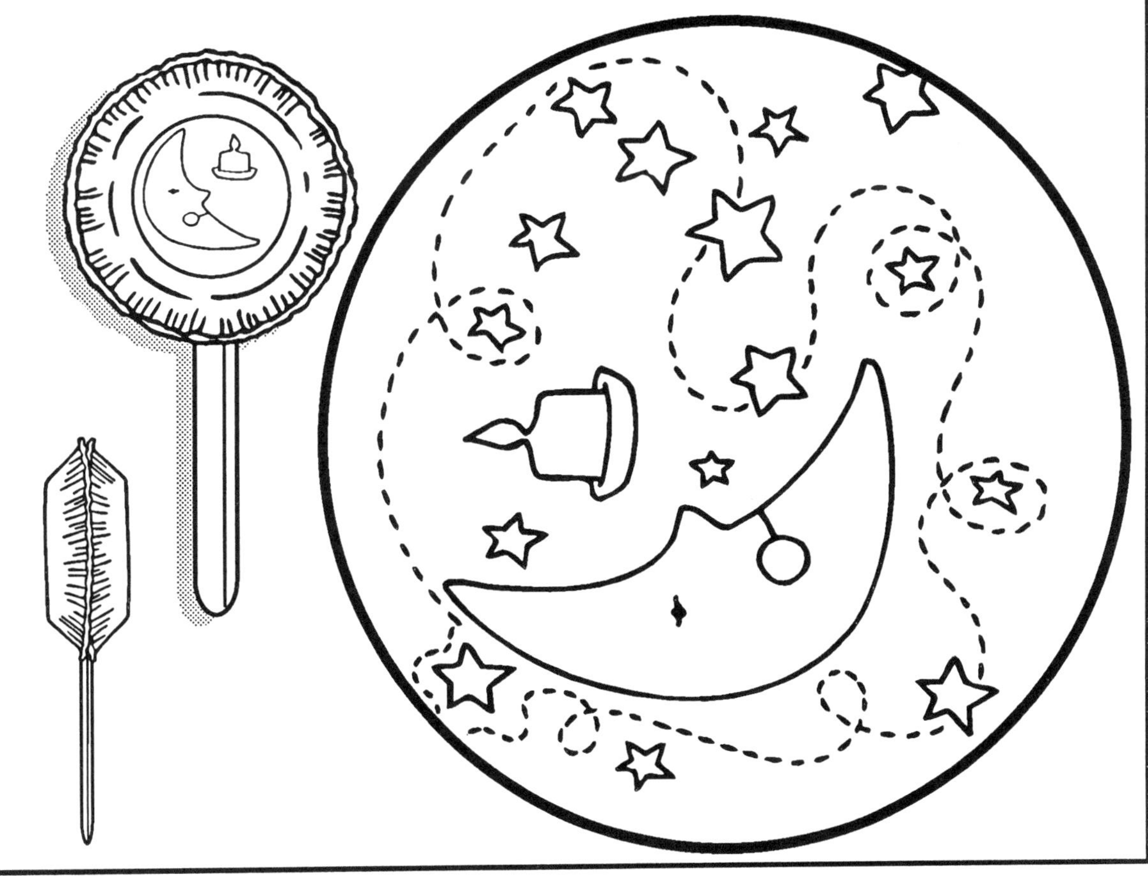

Moon Walk Drum

Each student will need an empty coffee can, scissors, glue, yarn, 2 wooden sticks, 2 red felt circles (3" or 7.62 cm diameter), cotton balls, and 2 drum wrappers (page 59).

1. Paint the drum wrapper patterns and allow to dry.
2. Cut out and apply glue to the back of each pattern.
3. Wrap the patterns around an empty coffee can.
4. Place two cotton balls in the center of a red felt circle.
5. Gather the circle and loosely tie a length of yarn around it as shown to form a pouch.
6. Apply glue to the end of a wooden stick and insert it in the center of the felt pouch.
7. Apply glue to the loose ends of yarn and tightly wrap them around the stick as shown.

Moon Walk Drum Wrapper

Moon Walk Headbands

Reproduce and provide each child in your class with the patterns on this page to make Moon Walk Headbands. Each child will need scissors, glue, glow-in-the-dark paint, a brush, and cellophane tape.

1. Paint the patterns and allow to dry.
2. Cut out and tape the patterns together to form one long strip.
3. Write your name on the back of the strip.
4. Wrap the strip around your head and tape it to fit.

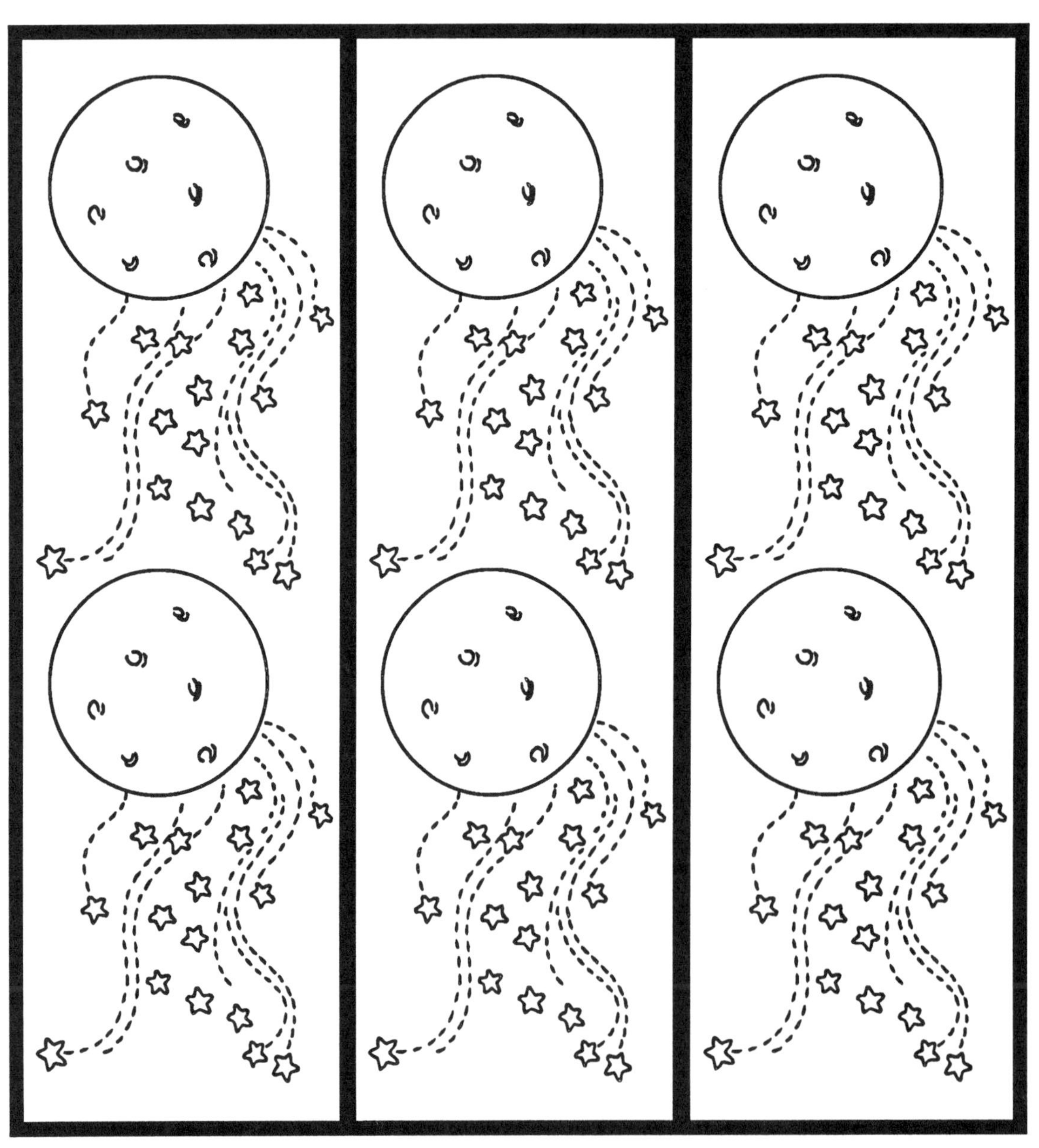

A TAKE-HOME NOTE FROM
ASIA

____
Date

Dear ______________________________,

We are ______________________________
______________________________.

Please ______________________________
____
____
____
____
____
____
____
____

____
____

Thank you!

____
Teacher

AUSTRALIA

Australia

Australia, originally the Australian States, was separate colonies of England. As a result, many Australian holidays and festivals are influenced by celebrations that originated in Great Britain.

Harvest Festivals

Australians celebrate harvest festivals in much the same manner as the British. However, because Australia's autumn occurs at a different time of the year, their celebrations take place during the months of March, April, and May.

Important harvest products include wheat, grains, fruits, and sheep, to name a few. Wool became very important in the late 1700s to early 1800s.

Have your students participate in a classroom agricultural harvest fair. Provide the patterns on pages 65-67 for children to create harvest display booths for judging. Your students will delight in making wooly sheep to display in a livestock booth with the patterns on pages 62-63. Invite parents to participate and attend your Australian Harvest Festival as part of your fall open house.

ORNAMENTS & DECORATIONS • AUSTRALIA
Wooly Sheep Fair

Stage a wooly sheep fair on your bulletin board. Cover your board with green paper and orange borders. Reproduce four fence patterns for each student in your class.

Use the take-home note on page 69 to ask for parent volunteers to help with this project. Ask volunteers to help reproduce, cut out, and punch holes as indicated in corrugated board patterns of the sheep and stand on page 63. Cut 3" (7.62 cm) lengths of gray, brown, and white yarn. Latch hook yarn may be substituted.

Provide students with yarn, crayons, and cellophane tape to assemble their wooly sheep.

1. Color, cut out, and assemble the fence patterns to make a pen for your sheep.
2. Write your name on the back of your sheep.
3. Tie a knot in one end of a length of yarn.
4. Thread the yarn from back to front through a hole in your sheep pattern.
5. Continue threading yarn through the remaining holes.
6. Attach the stand to your sheep and place it in the pen.

ORNAMENTS & DECORATIONS • AUSTRALIA

Wooly Sheep

Transfer sheep patterns onto poster or corrugated board. Punch a hole at each dot for students to thread lengths of yarn.

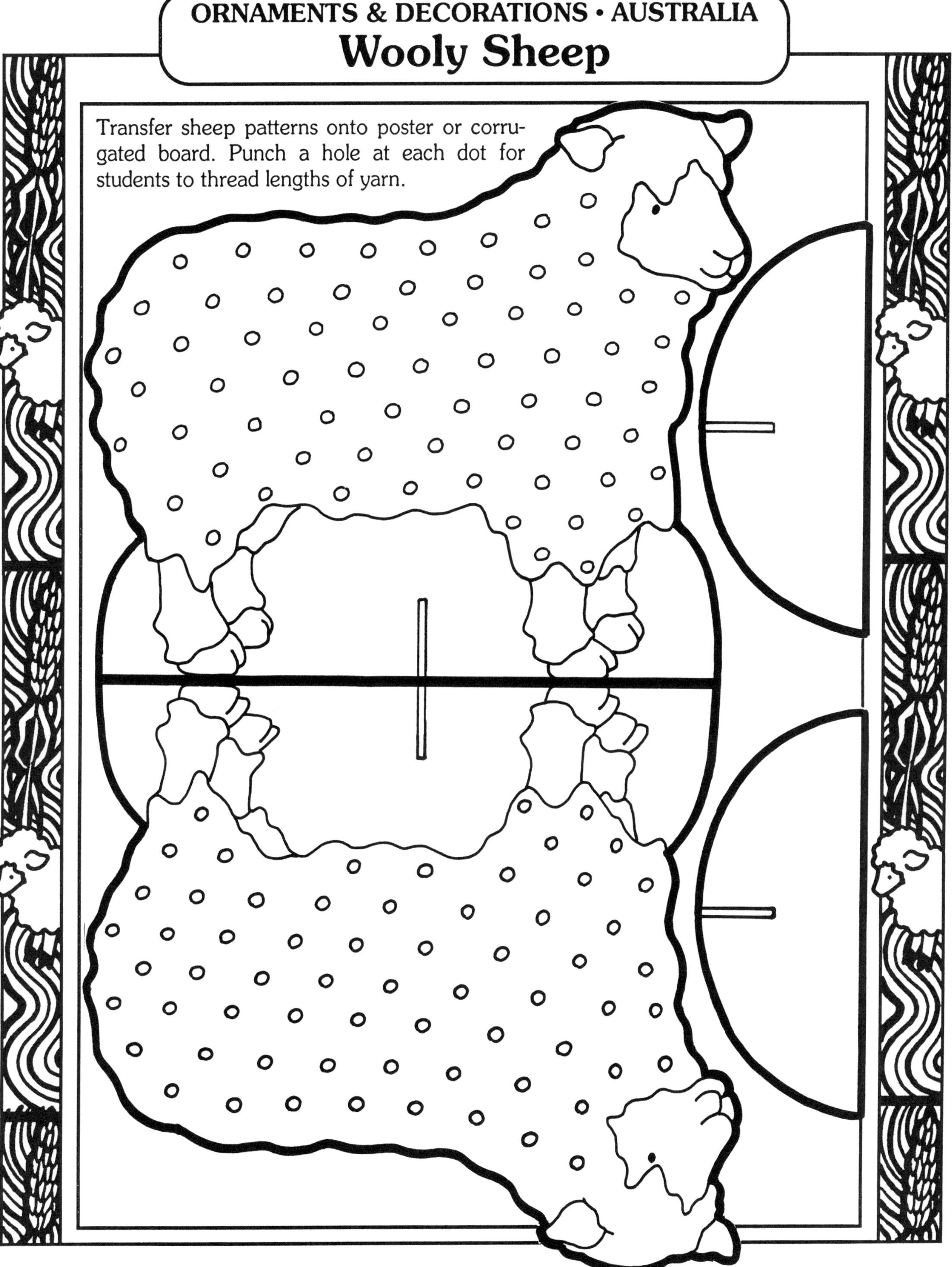

An Australian Harvest Festival

Provide students with the patterns on pages 65-67 and a sheet of colored construction paper to make harvest festival displays for your classroom.

Materials:
- crayons or markers
- scissors
- glue
- 12" x 18" (30.48 x 45.72 cm) sheet of construction paper
- a hole punch
- yarn

1. Color and cut out the cart and sign patterns.
2. Apply glue to the back of each cart pattern and attach to the sheet of construction paper.
3. Write your name or a harvest message on the sign.
4. Apply glue to the back of the sign and attach to the top of the cart.
5. Color and cut out the produce and basket patterns.
6. Arrange the patterns in the cart and glue in position.
7. Punch two holes at the top of your finished harvest cart.
8. Lace and tie a length of yarn through each hole and hang.

Harvest Patterns

Harvest Cart

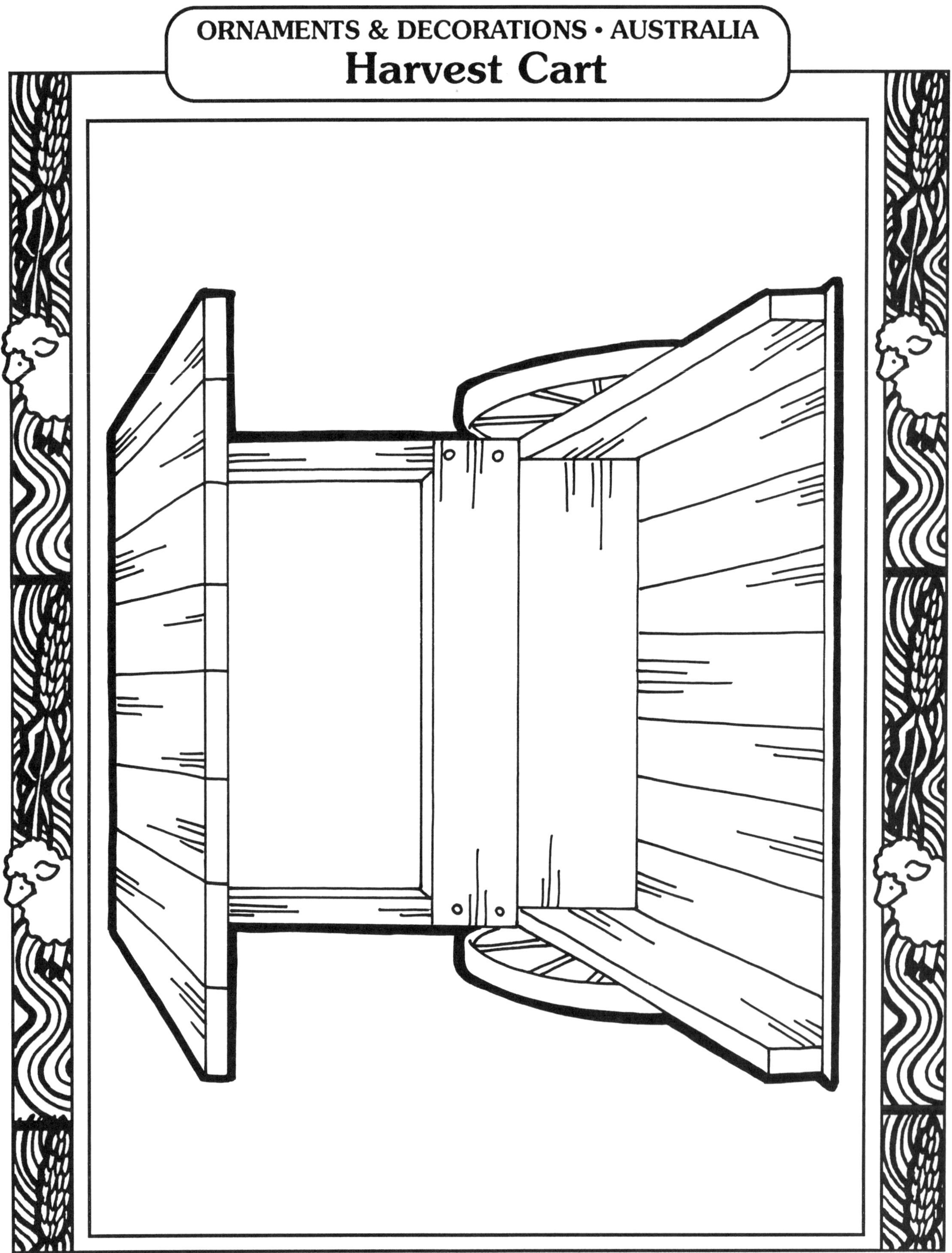

Harvest Cart

New Zealand

Big Muster

In New Zealand, farmers gather and move sheep from the mountains to warmer pastures for the winter. This is known as the *Big Muster*.

Guy Fawkes Day

Guy Fawkes Day is celebrated in a similar manner as in Great Britain, where this celebration originated.

Guy Fawkes, born in York, England, was involved in a plan to bring about the downfall of the government by lighting barrels of gunpowder stored in the cellar of Parliament. The plan failed when Guy Fawkes was found hiding in the cellar.

On November 5, children dress in rags, recite "Guy" rhymes, and ask for pennies, "A penny for the Guy, Mister?" This activity is similar to trick or treat on Halloween night. There are many versions of "Guy" rhymes. The following are a few lines from one:

> Please to remember the fifth of November,
> The gunpowder treason and plot.
> I see no reason why the gunpowder treason
> Should ever be forgot.

Invite your students to make up rhymes about Guy Fawkes Day. Have children write their rhymes on paper. Then provide each child with a sheet of colored construction paper and the coins below to decorate and mount on his or her rhyme. Display finished rhymes on the bulletin board.

A TAKE-HOME NOTE FROM
AUSTRALIA

____
Date

Dear ______________________,

We are ______________________
______________________.

Please ______________________
____
____
____
____
____
____
____
____
____
____

Thank you!

____
Teacher

EUROPE

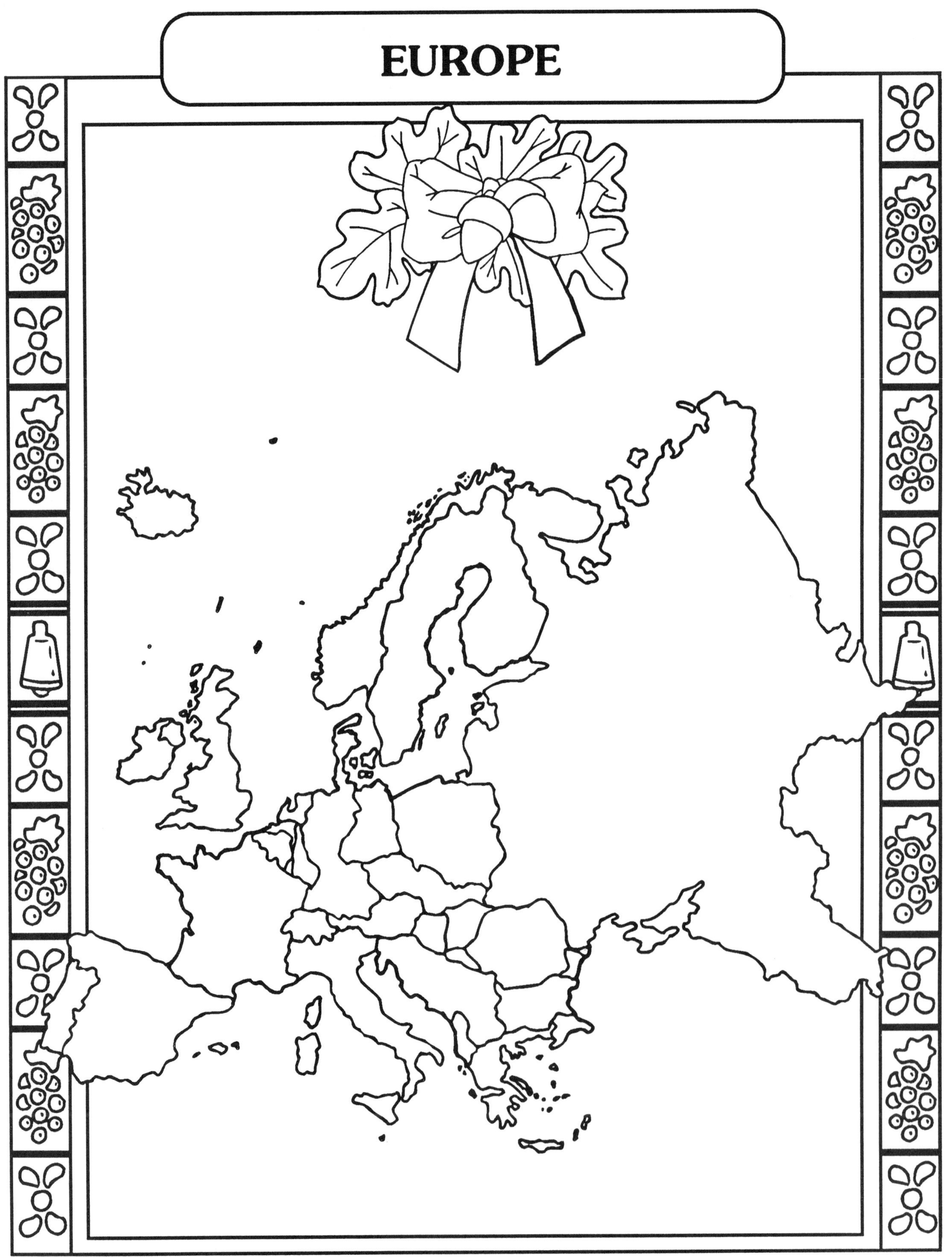

Europe

Austria

In Austria, cows are gathered and brought down from the Alpine pastures for the winter. The cows wear flower garlands laced with ribbons and the sound of cowbells rings through the villages as they pass.

Czechoslovakia

Straw, flowers, and corn are used to make a headdress wreath for the prettiest girl. She wears this wreath on *Obzinky*, a thanksgiving harvest festival. At the end of the harvest season, the girl and farm workers gather and enjoy music and song on their way to the landowner's home. Upon arriving at the landowner's home, the farmers offer him the wreath which is traditionally displayed in a place of honor until the next harvest. Meals enjoyed during the festival include roast pig; goose; and *kolaces*, square-shaped cakes filled with plum jam, cheese, or poppy seeds.

Denmark

In Denmark, harvesting corn is a kind of contest. Farmers work hard to harvest their crops making sure not to be the last one to finish. When all the fields are harvested the last and usually the tallest remaining stalk of corn is positioned in the field to mark the end of the harvest. Sometimes the stalk is dressed in clothes. Occasionally the last farmer to harvest his crops receives a "harvest helper" (a comical doll) from neighboring farmers.

At the end of the harvest all the farmers celebrate with a "harvest home" festival.

St. Martin's Day in Denmark

In Denmark, St. Martin's Day is a time for family reunions.

Alpine Cow Roundup

Use the take-home note on page 121 to ask for parents to send empty shoe boxes to school with students for Alpine Cow Roundup dioramas. Provide students with two sets of the pattern below, construction paper, scissors, and glue to complete this project.

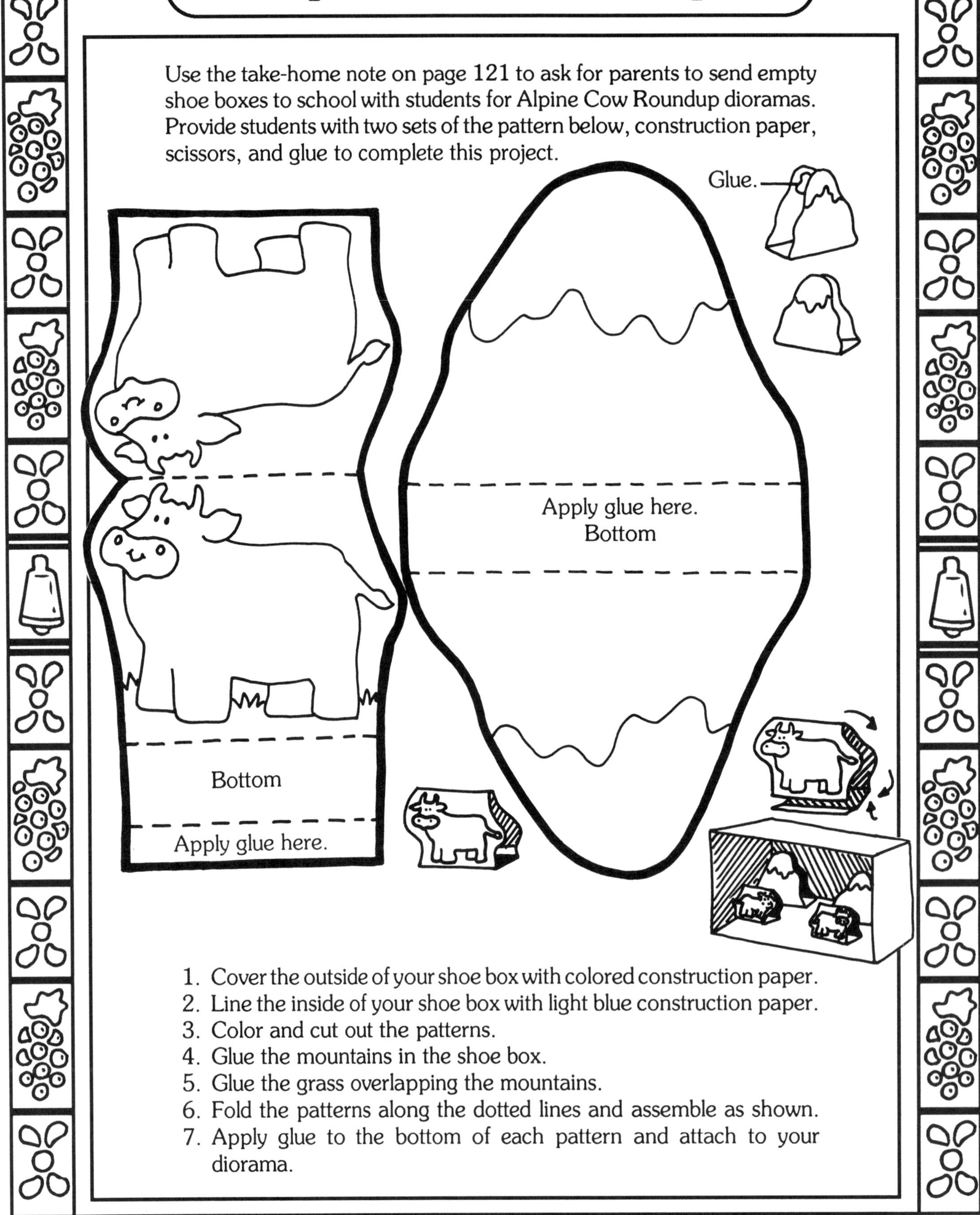

1. Cover the outside of your shoe box with colored construction paper.
2. Line the inside of your shoe box with light blue construction paper.
3. Color and cut out the patterns.
4. Glue the mountains in the shoe box.
5. Glue the grass overlapping the mountains.
6. Fold the patterns along the dotted lines and assemble as shown.
7. Apply glue to the bottom of each pattern and attach to your diorama.

HOLIDAY COOKING • CZECHOSLOVAKIA

A Kolace Treat

Children always enjoy afternoon snacks in the classroom. Prepare a table with bread squares, spreadable cream cheese, plum jam (substitute grape jelly if not available), paper plates, and utensils.

Provide each student with a toothpick, cellophane tape, and the goose pattern below to make kolace treat toppers.

1. Color and cut out the goose.
2. Write your name on the back.
3. Fold the pattern along the dotted line.
4. Open and apply glue to the back of the pattern.
5. Place a toothpick at the bottom edge as shown and fold.
6. Insert the goose topper in a triple decker cream cheese and jam kolace treat.

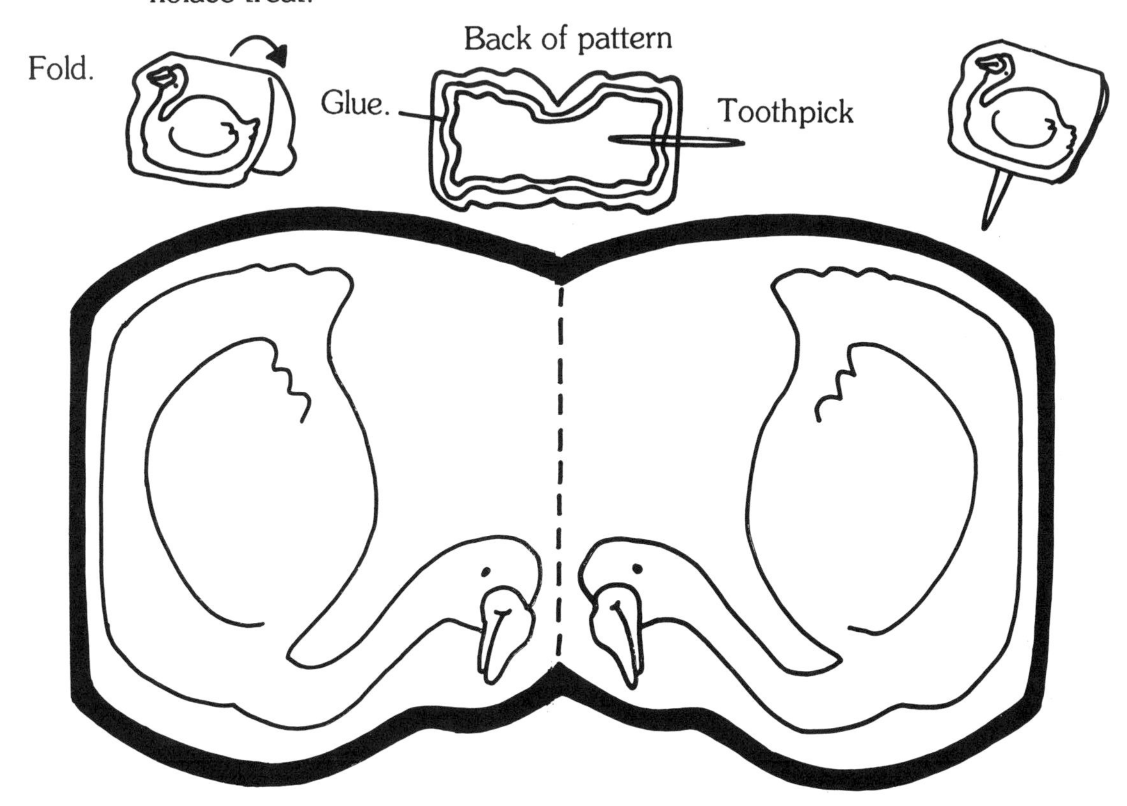

A Harvest Helper

Reproduce and provide the patterns on page 75 for students to make comical harvest helpers to display on the bulletin board. Cover the board with blue paper and autumn colored leaf borders. Write the title on a sign cut from a grocery bag to resemble wood.

Materials:
- patterns
- crayons or markers
- scissors
- glue

1. Color and cut out the patterns.
2. Draw a comical face on your harvest helper.
3. Glue the patterns together as shown.
4. Mount your harvest helper on the bulletin board.

A Harvest Helper

Europe

Finland

St. Michael's Day (Mikkelin paiva) is celebrated on the first Sunday in October in Finland. On this day the people gather to ask for a successful harvest. And workers are promised a job for the following year. Then candlelight dances are held to celebrate the end of the harvest.

France

Most crops ripen during the autumn months; however some crops ripen at other times. In France, lemons are harvested in February. The *Lemon Festival* takes place in the town of Mentone. A parade of lemon-filled wagons and lemon parade floats travels through streets lined with lemon, orange, grapefruit, and tangerine decorations.

Dancing by Candlelight

Provide students with two sets of the patterns below, crayons or markers, scissors, glue, and cellophane tape. Have students wear their candle headbands while dancing during a St. Michael's Day celebration.

1. Color and cut out the patterns.
2. Tape the headband strips together.
3. Apply glue to the headband strips where indicated.
4. Attach the candles to the headband.
5. Wrap the headband around your head to fit and secure with tape.

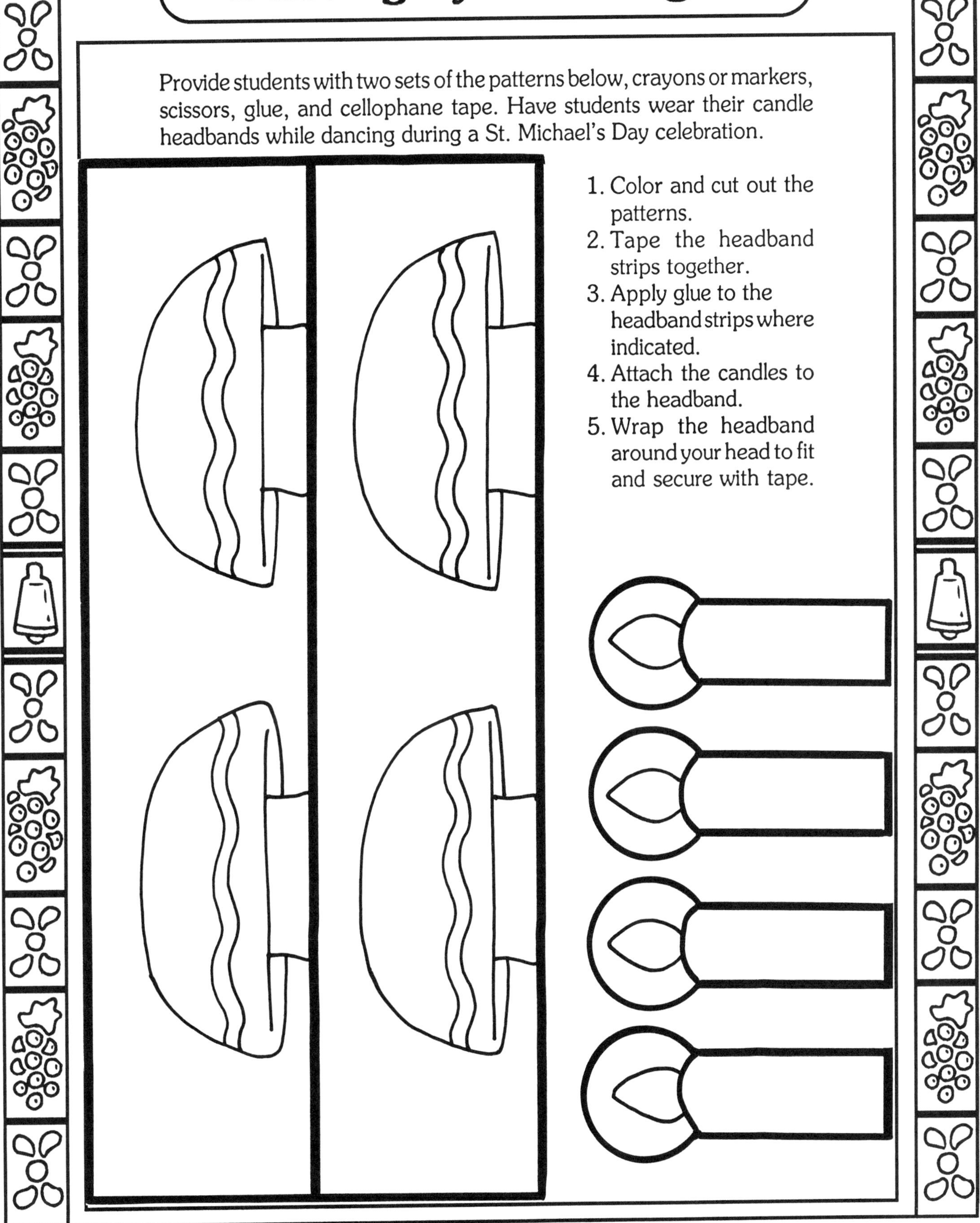

ORNAMENTS & DECORATIONS • FRANCE

Lemon Parade Hats

Reproduce and provide each child in your class with the patterns below to make Lemon Festival hats. Provide paper plates, crayons or markers, scissors, glue, yarn, and a hole punch. Punch a hole on opposite sides of the paper plate and attach yarn ties.

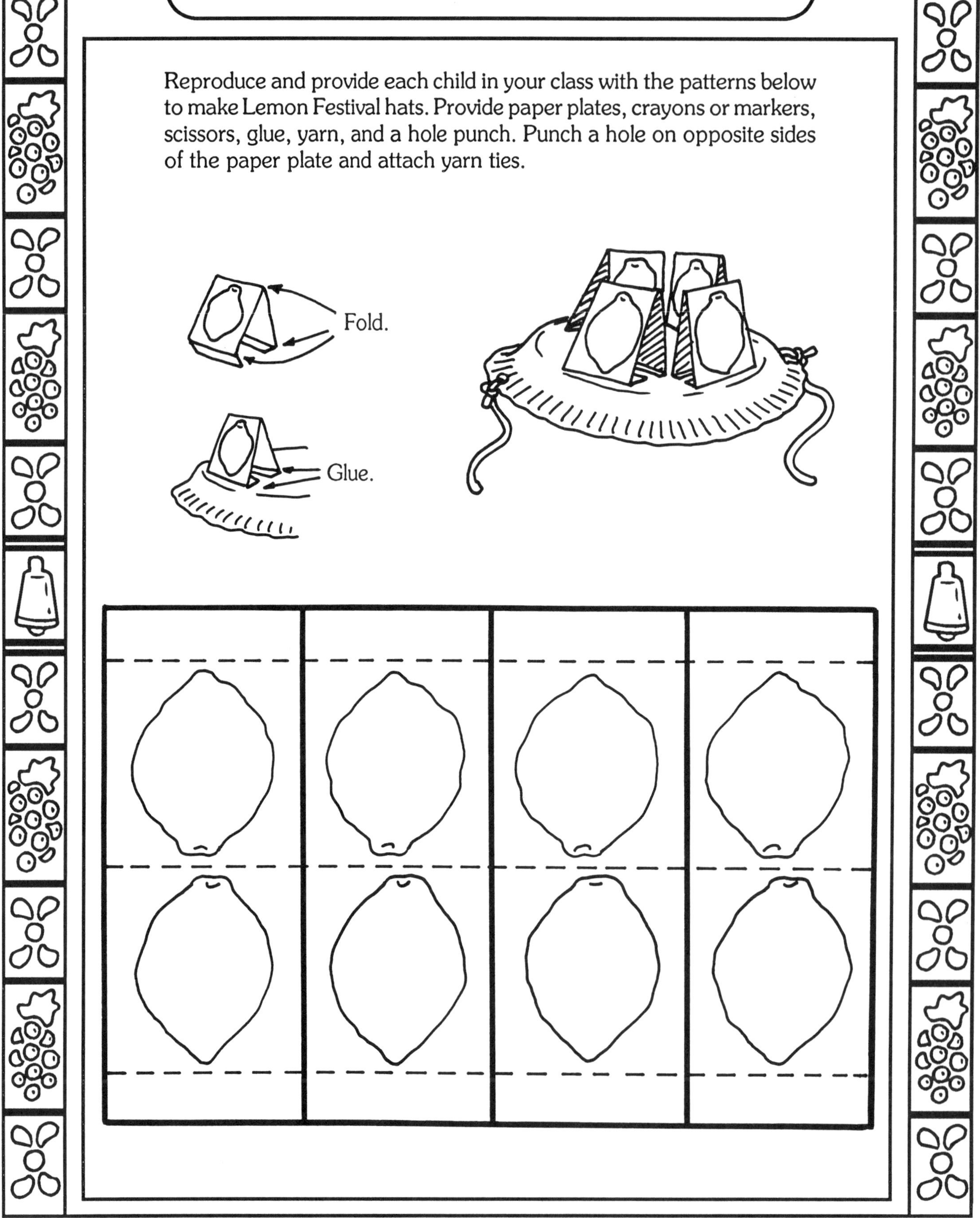

Germany

Oktoberfest

Every year the Germans enjoy a lively autumn festival called *Oktoberfest* in the city of Munich. The festival features folk dancers and singers, and displays of harvested farm products. Everyone has plenty to eat and drink.

St. Martin's Day

In Germany, St. Martin's Day is called *Martinstag*. Martin of Tours, who was to be named a prominent religious leader, unsuccessfully hid among a flock of geese because he felt unworthy. He was discovered when the geese cackled. Today, restaurants serve *Martinsgans* (goose) in memory of this event.

Children once made lanterns, similar to jack-o'-lanterns, to participate in lantern parades. The lanterns lit the way as children traveled the streets singing and reciting rhymes. Today, the children of Germany continue the tradition of lantern parades. However, the lanterns are made of paper and the festivities are not necessarily associated with St. Martin.

ORNAMENTS & DECORATIONS • GERMANY

Oktoberfest Carton Wrapper

Prepare an Oktoberfest snack of milk and gingerbread cookies for your class. Provide students with crayons or markers, scissors, cellophane tape, and the pictures below. Show how to tape the pictures around a milk carton.

1. Color and cut out the pictures.
2. Tape the pictures around a milk carton.

St. Martin's Day Lanterns

Organize a lantern parade with your class. Provide children with the patterns and materials listed below to make pumpkin lanterns. Hang additional lanterns in the classroom.

1. Color and cut out the pattern.
2. Fold the pattern as shown below.
3. Apply glue to the tab and assemble the lantern.
4. Punch a hole at each dot.
5. Lace and tie a length of yarn through each hole.
6. Tie the loose ends together.

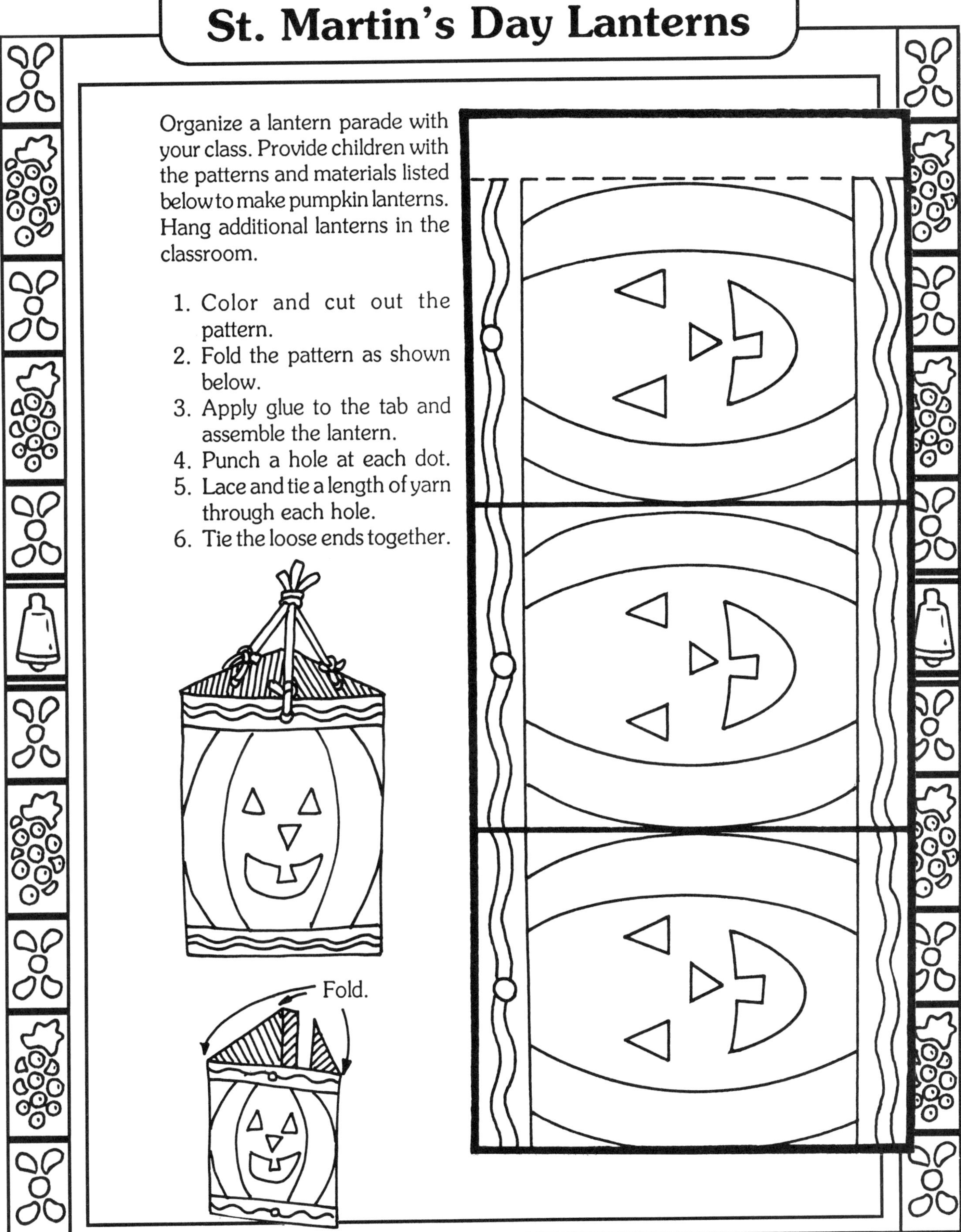

Great Britain

Guy Fawkes Day

On November 5, bonfires, fireworks, and children dressed in ragged clothes fill the streets of England. Children carry dummies through the streets shouting, "A penny for the old Guy!" The dummies are stuffed with straw or paper and always wear top hats.

The activities of this day remind the people of England of a historical event. Early in the seventeenth century, Guy Fawkes and others planned to destroy Parliament, an English government building and body of lawmakers. The plan failed when Guy Fawkes was discovered in the cellar of Parliament with gunpowder, a tinder box, and matches.

Every year on the anniversary of this historical event, the Royal Guardsmen, dressed in their traditional costumes, carry lanterns to search the cellar of the House of Parliament.

This celebration also takes place in countries with strong English influence such as Australia.

Halloween

Great Britain celebrates Halloween or All Hallow's Eve on October 31. This celebration is often combined with Guy Fawkes Day. The celebration lasts for a week ending with a fireworks display on bonfire night.

Children dress in costumes, participate in mischief, sing Halloween songs (a favorite custom), play games, and trick-or-treat. Traditional foods include pumpkin pie, turnips, chestnuts, flapjacks, toffee apples, baked potatoes, and hot dogs. Mischief during the holiday celebration is all in fun, hedge-hopping and cat-walking (sneaking across hedges and around the outside of houses).

Bob Apple is a favorite traditional game. Another game, slightly different from Bob Apple involves apples hanging from the ceiling rather than floating in a tub of water. However, the goal is the same, to catch the apples using only your mouth.

Guy Fawkes Theater

Invite your students to help write a puppet theater production about Guy Fawkes. Enlarge the theater patterns on pages 84 and 85. Color, cut out, and attach the patterns to poster board for a theater backdrop. Reproduce the puppet patterns on page 86 and glue to Popsicle™ sticks for students to use during a Guy Fawkes Day production.

Guy Fawkes Theater

Guy Fawkes Theater

Guy Fawkes Theater Puppets

A Bob Apple Game

You will need large paper clips, magnetic tape, yarn, plastic straws, and the apple patterns on page 88 for students to participate in a game of Bob Apple.

1. Reproduce and attach a large paper clip to each apple.
2. Punch a hole at the top of each apple.
3. Lace and tie a length of yarn to each apple and mount on your bulletin board.
4. Provide a plastic straw with magnetic tape attached to one end for each child in your class.
5. In turn, have each child hold a straw between his or her teeth and try to snag an apple.
6. Reward children who succeed with a sticker or other prize.

A Bob Apple Game

Guy Fawkes Hand Puppet

Reproduce and provide students with gray, black, and pink felt and the patterns below to make their own hand puppets for a British Halloween festival. Also provide scissors, fabric glue, and permanent black markers.

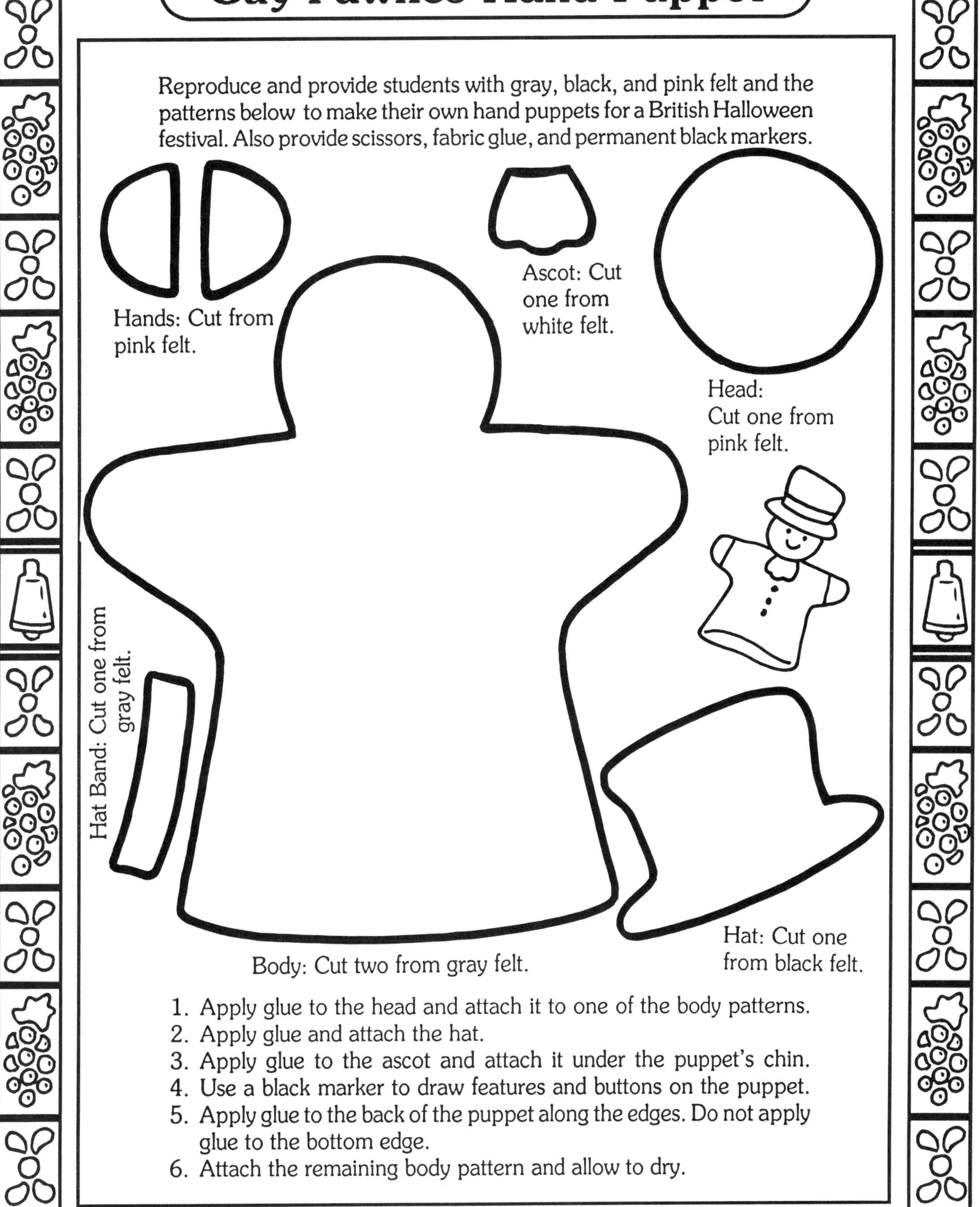

1. Apply glue to the head and attach it to one of the body patterns.
2. Apply glue and attach the hat.
3. Apply glue to the ascot and attach it under the puppet's chin.
4. Use a black marker to draw features and buttons on the puppet.
5. Apply glue to the back of the puppet along the edges. Do not apply glue to the bottom edge.
6. Attach the remaining body pattern and allow to dry.

Great Britain

Harvest Festivals

Harvest festivals in Great Britain were once held in fields and barns. Today, religious services are closely associated with the celebration, and many celebrations begin with thanksgiving services in a church (a building for public worship). Schools also hold harvest festivals and follow the tradition of distributing produce from the season's harvest to local charities. Decorations include stalks of wheat, fruits, vegetables, and flowers.

Harvest Home

In England food from the harvest is shared with the needy. Sometimes notes are tucked in harvest baskets. This custom is known as *Harvest Home*.

Michaelmas

Michaelmas, named after a famous dragon fighter, St. Michael, is known as the fall season in England. This holiday, originally a medieval celebration, is filled with three delights—glove, goose, and ginger.

In September, a giant glove is hung from a pole in a prominent location in town. Goose and ginger, believed to bring good luck and good health, are served during the fair. *Chardwardon* is a ginger-flavored dessert made with pears, sugar, cinnamon, nutmeg, and ginger.

Harvest Home Baskets

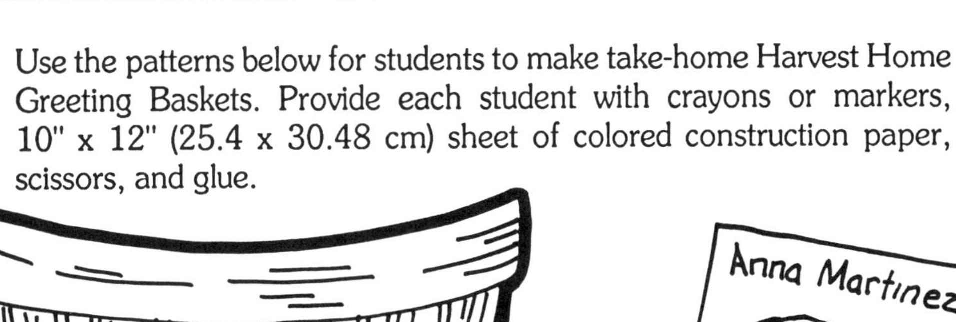

Use the patterns below for students to make take-home Harvest Home Greeting Baskets. Provide each student with crayons or markers, 10" x 12" (25.4 x 30.48 cm) sheet of colored construction paper, scissors, and glue.

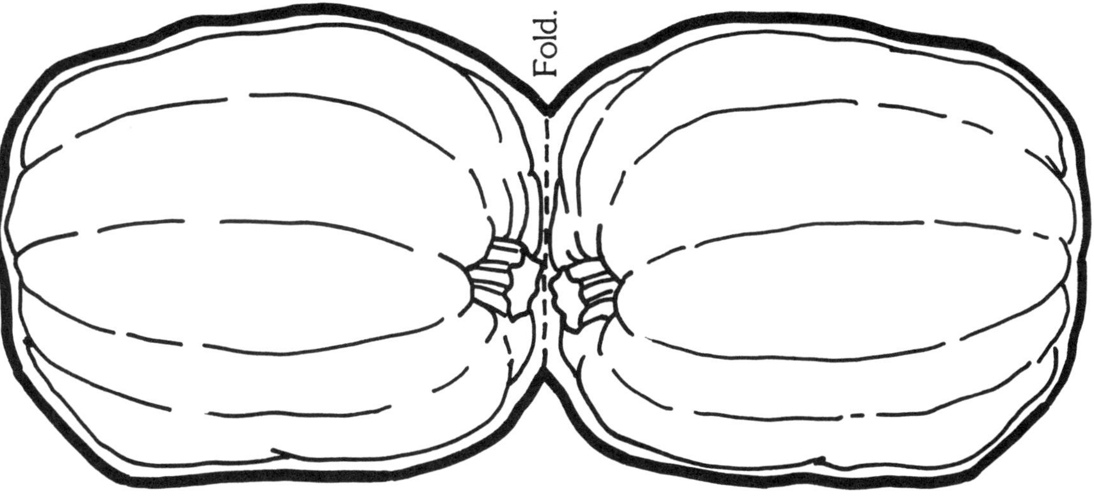

1. Color and cut out the patterns.
2. Apply glue to the back of your basket along the edges. Do not apply glue to the top of the basket.
3. Attach the basket to a sheet of construction paper.
4. Fold the card along the dotted line.
5. Write harvest greetings inside the card.
6. Insert the card in the basket.
7. Write your name at the top.

Michaelmas Glove Garland

Reproduce these patterns for students to make garlands to decorate your classroom for a Michaelmas celebration. Provide crayons or markers, scissors, glue, glitter, and a variety of craft supplies. Have children punch two holes at the wristband. Thread yarn or bright-colored ribbon through each hole. Continue adding gloves in this manner.

Gingerbread Dragon Fighter

The patterns on pages 93 and 94 will delight young students. Share the story of St. Michael with your class. Then provide students with the dragon and dragon fighter patterns to make Michaelmas pictures to display on your bulletin board. Reproduce the patterns on brown construction paper or brown grocery bags. Provide each child with crayons or markers, white chalk, scissors, glue, and a 12" x 18" (30.48 x 45.72 cm) sheet of construction paper.

Gingerbread Dragon

Great Britain

Mop Fair

The *Mop Fair* is a festival that takes place in the town of Stratford-on-Avon at the end of the harvest season. Its origin dates back to when farm helpers were hired by the year. At the end of the harvest season employers and helpers both traveled to town, one looking for help, the other looking for new work. Those seeking new work would carry their tools to show what they could do. The festival gets its name from the mops carried by women who were also looking for new work. Everyone enjoyed performances by musicians, eating food, and shopping.

Today the fair opens with a festival official, wearing a red coat, ringing a bell and the mayor, dressed in a long black robe and a tall silk hat, greeting the crowd. Visitors enjoy rides, buying souvenirs, and eating special foods.

Punkie Night

Punkie Night is traditionally celebrated on the fourth Thursday in October. The activities of this night are similar to those of Halloween.

One legend tells the story of a group of men who went to a fair in a nearby town. On their return home it was so dark that they placed candles in hollowed vegetables to use as lanterns to light their way.

Today children make lanterns from a variety of hollowed vegetables to light their way as they sing from house to house asking for pennies.

Mop Fair Bulletin Board

Have your students participate in a Mop Fair in your classroom. Enlarge and reproduce the patterns below for students to color and cut out. Have children write their names on the back of the mops. Invite them to write a sentence about what services they will be selling at the Mop Fair on oaktag sentence strips.

Punkie Night Lanterns

Reproduce the patterns below for students to make Punkie Night Lanterns. Provide crayons, scissors, glue, a hole punch, and yarn. Display the lanterns as Halloween draws near.

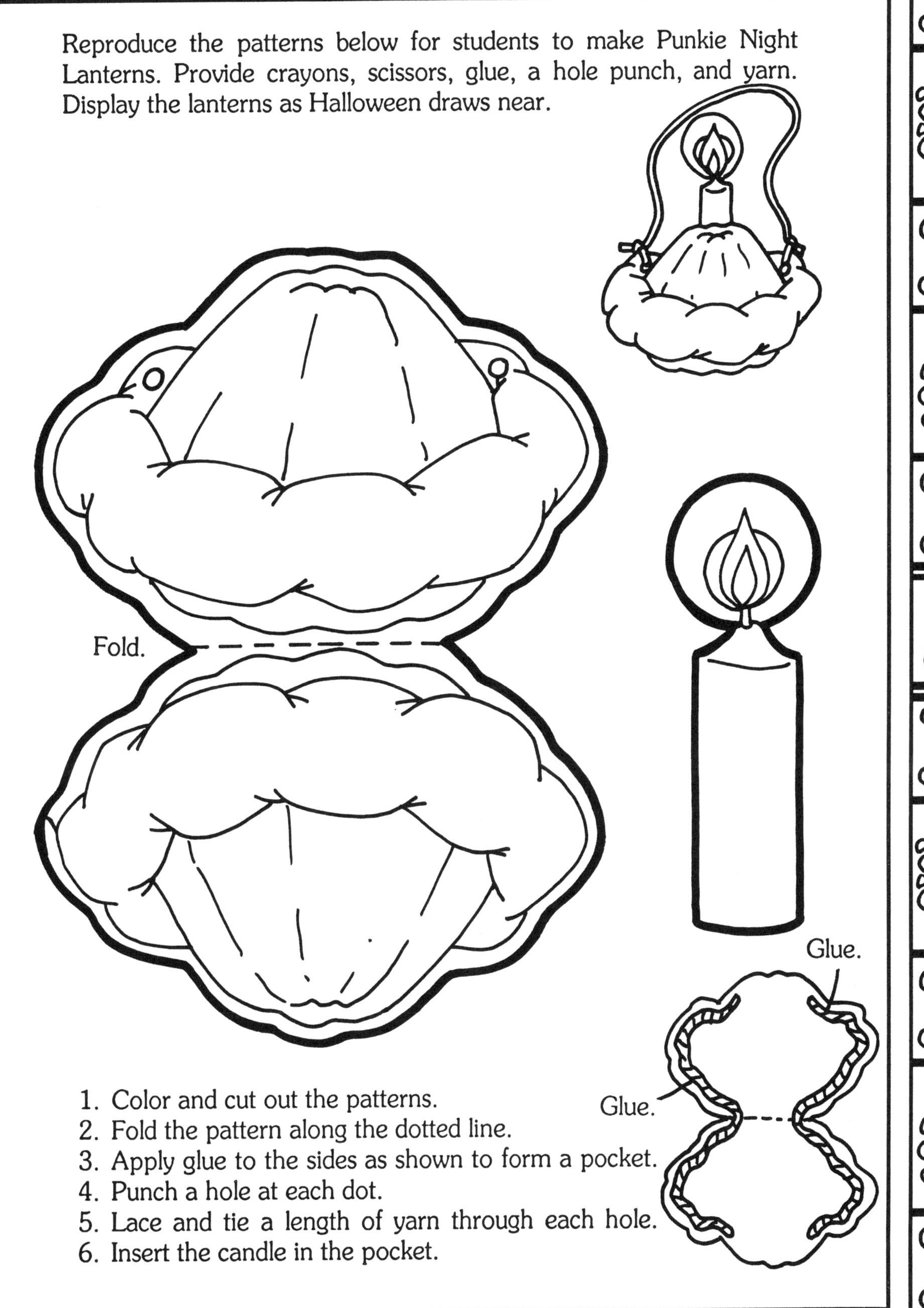

1. Color and cut out the patterns.
2. Fold the pattern along the dotted line.
3. Apply glue to the sides as shown to form a pocket.
4. Punch a hole at each dot.
5. Lace and tie a length of yarn through each hole.
6. Insert the candle in the pocket.

Great Britain

St. Crispin's Day

St. Crispin's Day, originally a popular medieval festival, occurs during the month of October in honor of St. Crispin, one of two shoemaker brothers. Because this holiday occurs a few days before Halloween, the two holidays are often celebrated together. However, it is "King" Crispin who presides over the festival.

Everyone dresses in medieval costumes and pretends to be a member of King Crispin's court. Each guest wears a purple baldric (a leather belt worn across the chest) with a gold shoe painted on it. Only seven guests wear masks. These masked guests carry baskets to collect treats from the guests. In the tradition of trick or treat, guests who do not give treats are threatened with amusing punishments.

King Crispin sits at the head table. He carries a staff and wears an elaborate robe, a medallion with a shoe design on a gold chain, and a crown. Tables are decorated with fruit and jack-o'-lanterns (hollowed turnips and squash). The guests share a festive meal and participate in games such as apple bobbing.

The festival ends with a candlelight procession. Guests carrying candles in hollowed apple candle holders circle the room three times, each time bowing to King Crispin as they pass in front of him.

Celebrate St. Crispin's Day with your class. Reproduce the patterns on pages 99-101 for King Crispin, his royal court, and seven masked trick-or-treaters. Provide each child in your class with materials to make purple baldrics and candles to carry during the candlelight procession.

King Crispin's Crown

Use the pattern below to prepare a crown for one of your students to wear. Attach the medallion to the center of the crown as shown. Invite students to vote for King Crispin.

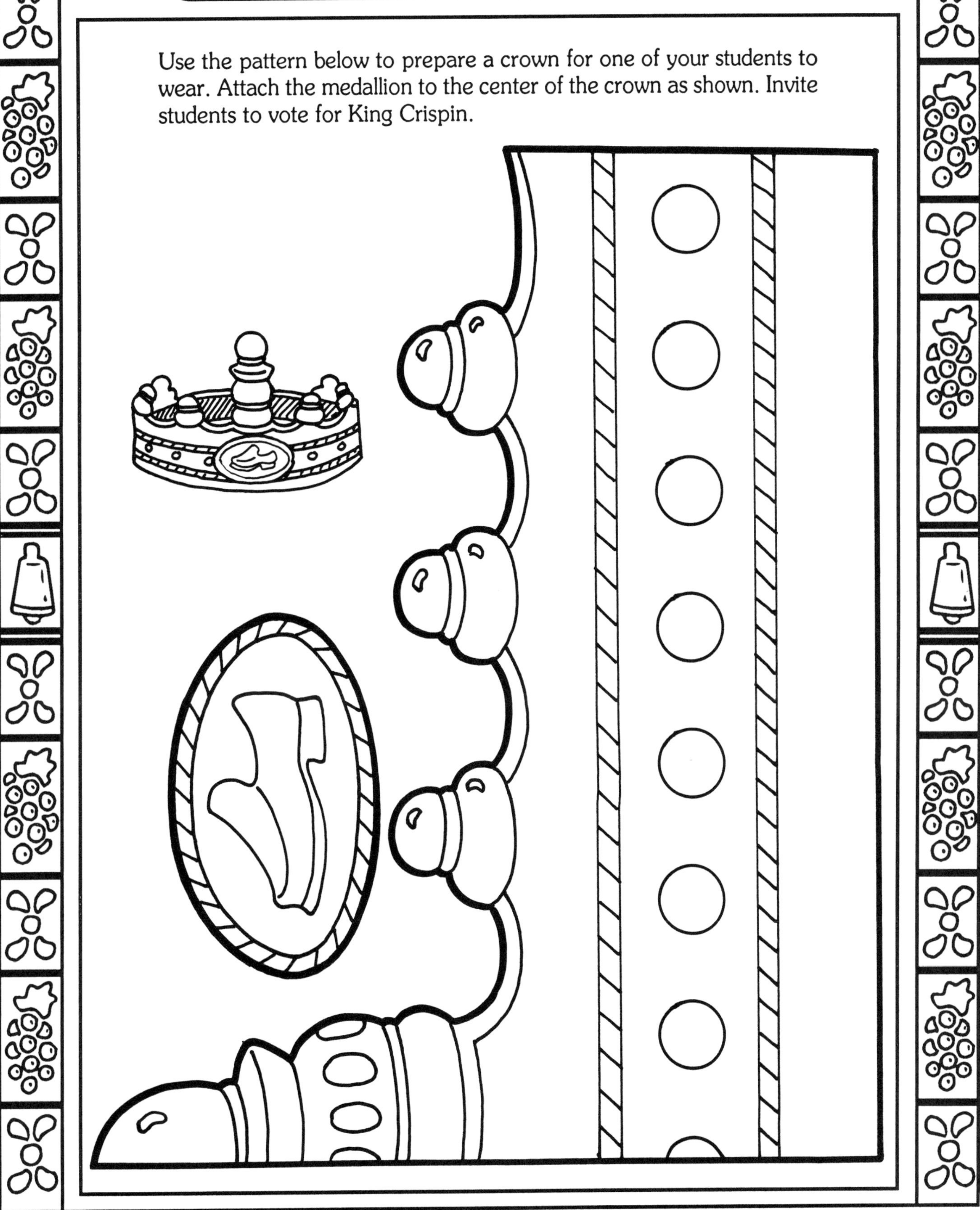

King Crispin's Medallion & Staff

Materials:
- crayons or markers
- scissors
- glue
- a yardstick
- yellow and orange construction paper
- yellow and orange crepe paper streamers

Staff

1. Reproduce the staff ornament and medallion on yellow construction paper or poster board.
2. Wrap a yardstick with yellow and orange construction paper strips or crepe paper streamers.
3. Apply glue and attach the staff ornament to one end of the yardstick.

Medallion

1. Punch a hole at each dot on the medallion.
2. Lace and tie a length of yarn or gold ribbon through the holes.

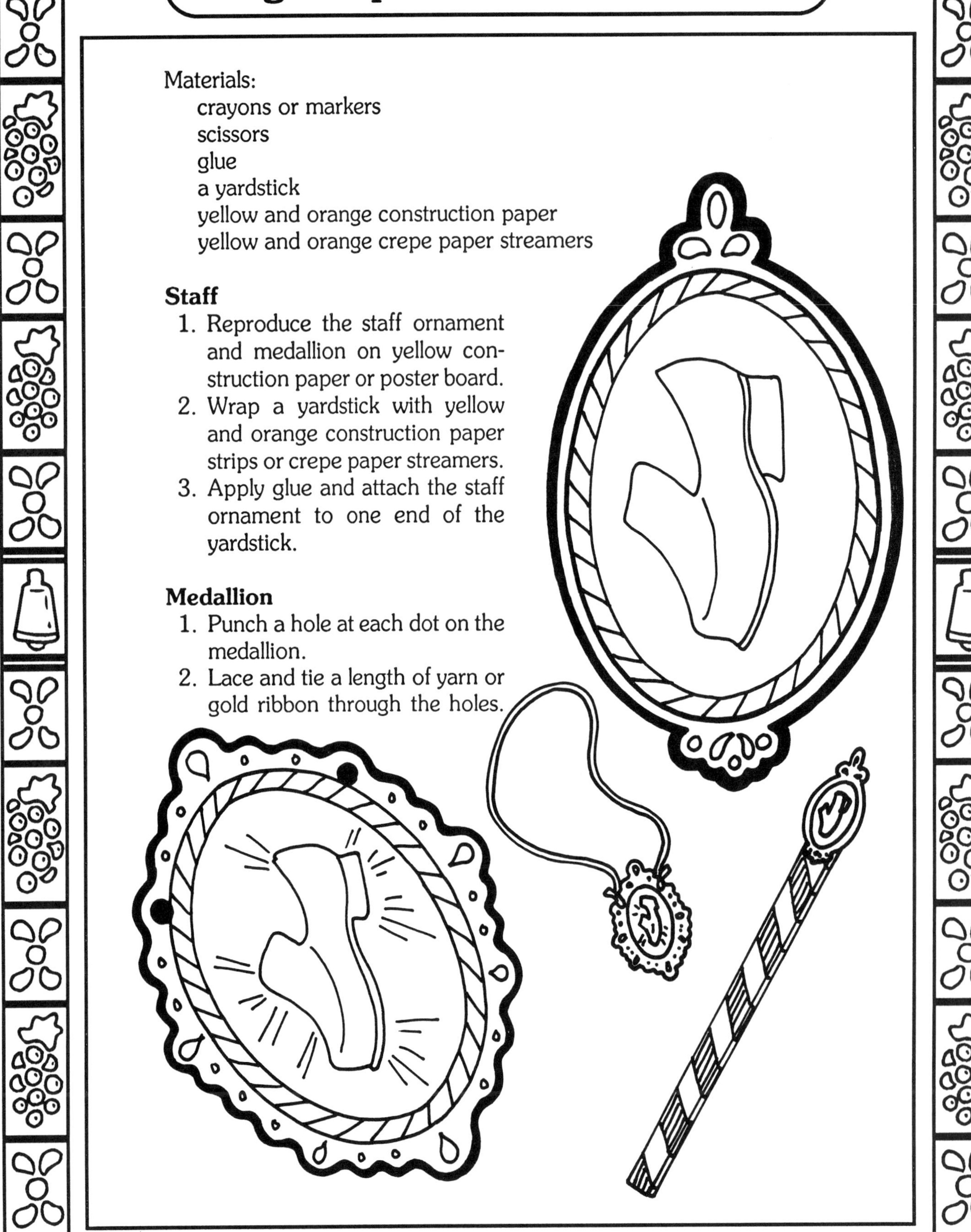

Crispin's Mask & Baldric

Materials:
- 4" x 18" (10.16 x 45.72 cm) purple construction paper strips
- crayons or markers
- scissors
- glue
- yarn
- a hole punch
- a stapler

Mask
1. Color and cut out the mask.
2. Punch a hole on each side of the mask.
3. Lace and tie a length of yarn through each hole.

Baldric
1. Decorate three purple construction paper strips.
2. Apply glue to the back of each medallion and attach it to the strips.
3. Use a stapler to join the strips together to form a baldric.
4. Wear the baldric over one shoulder as shown.

HOLIDAY TRADITIONS & LEGENDS

Europe

Ireland

The people of Ireland enjoy traditional holiday meals and play games on Halloween night. Strawboys (boys dressed in white straw costumes) dance with girls in kitchens. The best apples and ripened nuts are picked for *Snap Apple Night*, and preparations are made for the long winter.

Jack-o'-lanterns are believed to have originated from an old Irish tale. A man named Jack, who had nowhere to go after death, hollowed out a turnip to hold a hot coal to light his way in search of a place to rest. Originally children carved faces in turnips and potatoes and hollowed them to hold candles. Today pumpkins replace the turnips and potatoes.

Italy

Joust of the Saracen, or Giostra del Saracino, is celebrated on the first Sunday in September. Dressed as knights in shining armor, participants compete in thirteenth-century tilting contests. Tilting is a jousting contest. Two knights mounted on horses engage in combat with lances. A lance is a medieval weapon, a long pole fitted with a sharp metal head.

Giostra della Quintana, a revival of a seventeenth-century event, is also celebrated in September. Six hundred costumed knights participate in a jousting contest on the second Sunday in September.

Lithuania

The festival of *Nubaigai*, or Grain Harvest, is celebrated in Lithuania. The celebration includes dancing and singing and a variety of traditional customs.

At the end of the harvest, the last sheath is usually dressed like an old woman known as a *Boba* and presented to the farmer at his home. The farmer traditionally soaks the Boba with water to bring good luck for the next harvest.

A wreath covered with cloth is placed on a plate as a gift to the farmer. A young girl carries the wreath and leads the parade to the farmer's home. The farmer thanks everyone and presents a gift to each girl in the parade.

Strawboy Pockets

Materials:
- construction paper
- 1/2 paper plate
- crayons or markers
- scissors
- glue
- a stapler

1. Color and cut out the pattern.
2. Glue the pattern to a sheet of construction paper.
3. Staple 1/2 of a paper plate at the bottom of the pattern.
4. Write your name on the pocket.

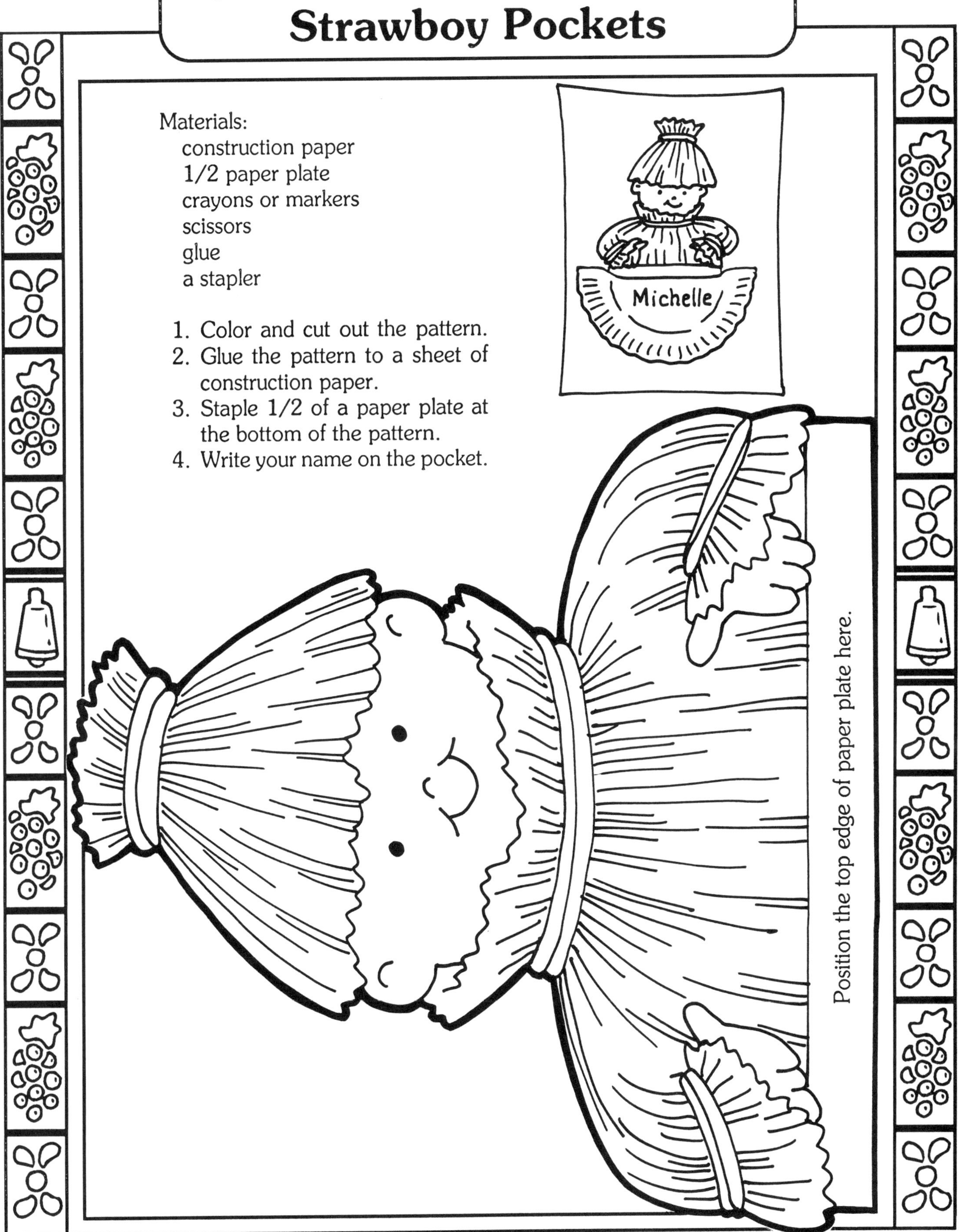

Jousting Puppets

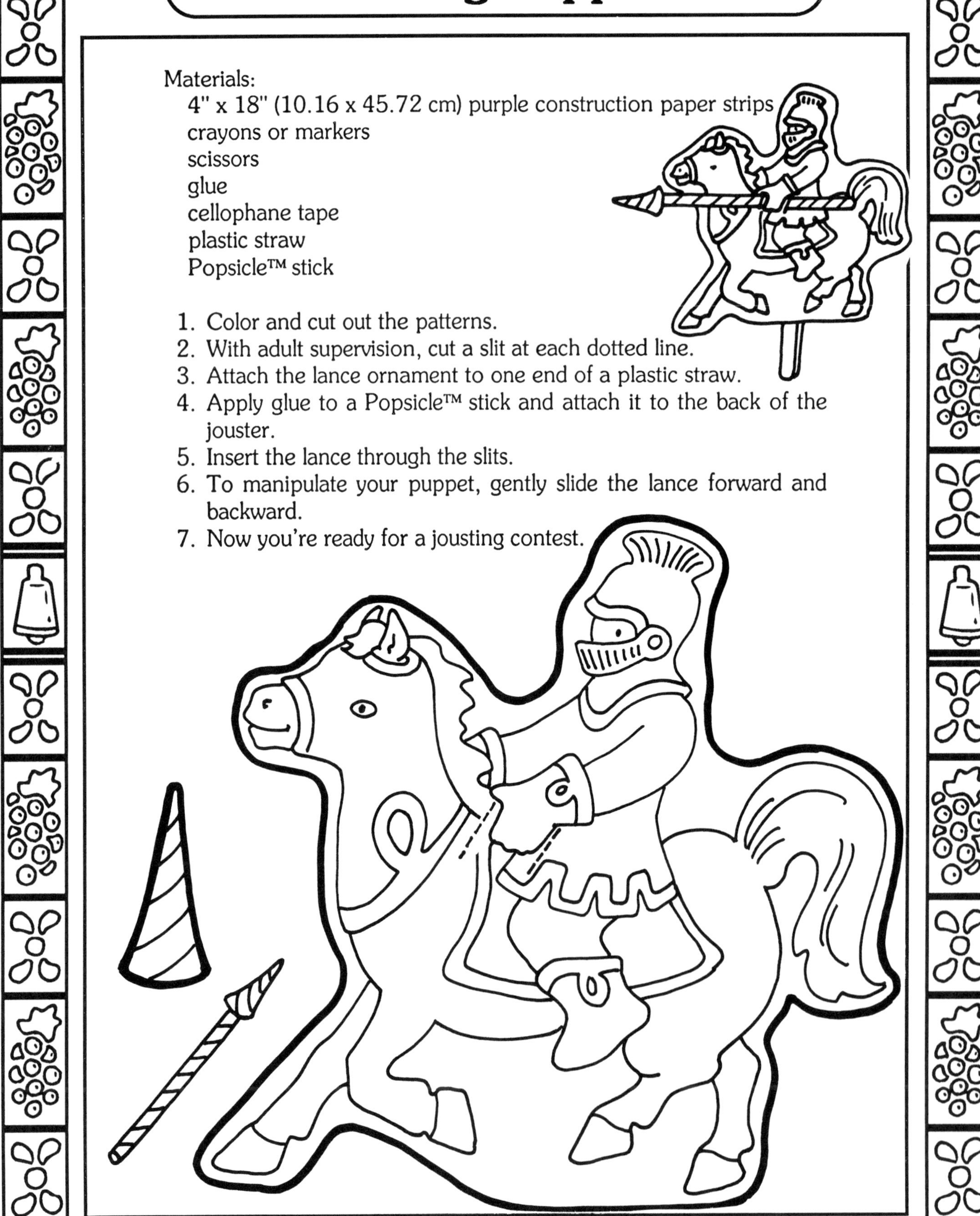

Materials:

4" x 18" (10.16 x 45.72 cm) purple construction paper strips
crayons or markers
scissors
glue
cellophane tape
plastic straw
Popsicle™ stick

1. Color and cut out the patterns.
2. With adult supervision, cut a slit at each dotted line.
3. Attach the lance ornament to one end of a plastic straw.
4. Apply glue to a Popsicle™ stick and attach it to the back of the jouster.
5. Insert the lance through the slits.
6. To manipulate your puppet, gently slide the lance forward and backward.
7. Now you're ready for a jousting contest.

ORNAMENTS & DECORATIONS • LITHUANIA

Nubaigai Bulletin Board & Gifts

Decorate your classroom bulletin board for a Lithuanian harvest festival. Reproduce, color, and cut out the gift and sheath patterns on page 107. Mount the patterns on the board. Add student-made Good Luck Bobas (page 106) to complete this festive display.

NUBAIGAI

A Grain Harvest Festival

Good Luck Boba

Substitute twisted craft ribbon (available at craft stores) for corn husks for students to make these delightful Good Luck Bobas. Provide each child with a scarf cut from cloth scraps, 2 lengths of twisted craft ribbon, yarn, glue, a cotton ball, and colored markers. Solicit parent volunteers to unravel craft ribbon and help students with this project.

1. Fold a 12" (30.48 cm) length of craft ribbon in half.
2. Twist the craft ribbon 2" (5.08 cm) from the folded end and tie a length of yarn to form a head and body.
3. Use colored markers to add facial features and designs to the body.
4. Twist the ends of a 6" (15.24 cm) length of craft ribbon and tie a length of yarn to each end to form the boba's arms.
5. Position the arms in back of the boba's body as shown.
6. Secure the arms with a length of yarn. Crisscross and tie the yarn as shown.
7. Insert a cotton ball in the head.
8. Cut short lengths of yarn and attach to the boba's head with glue.
9. Tie a cloth scarf to the boba's head.

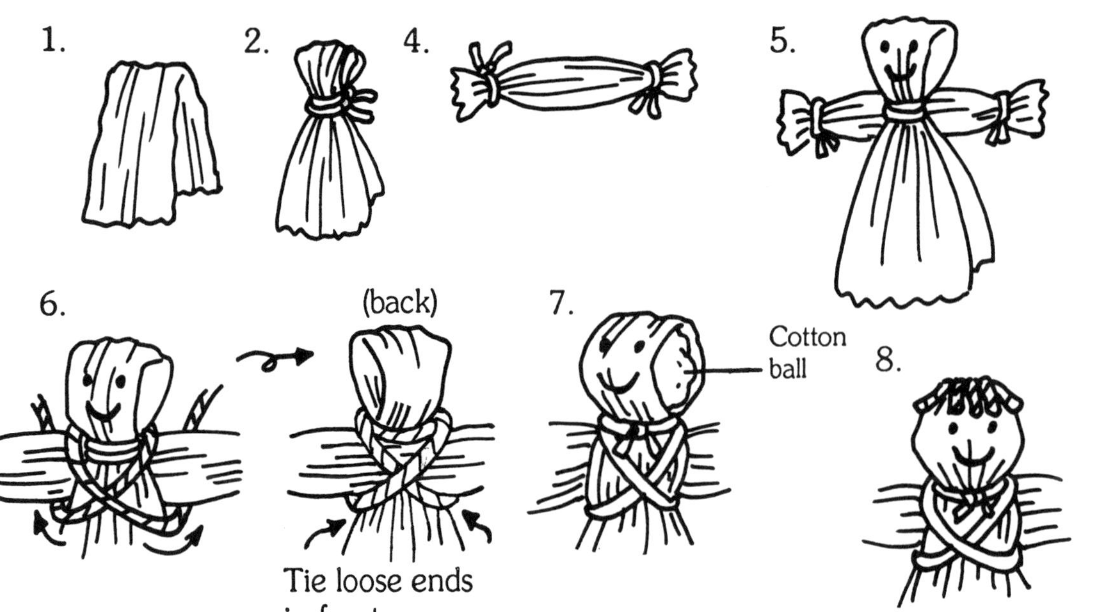

Harvest Sheath

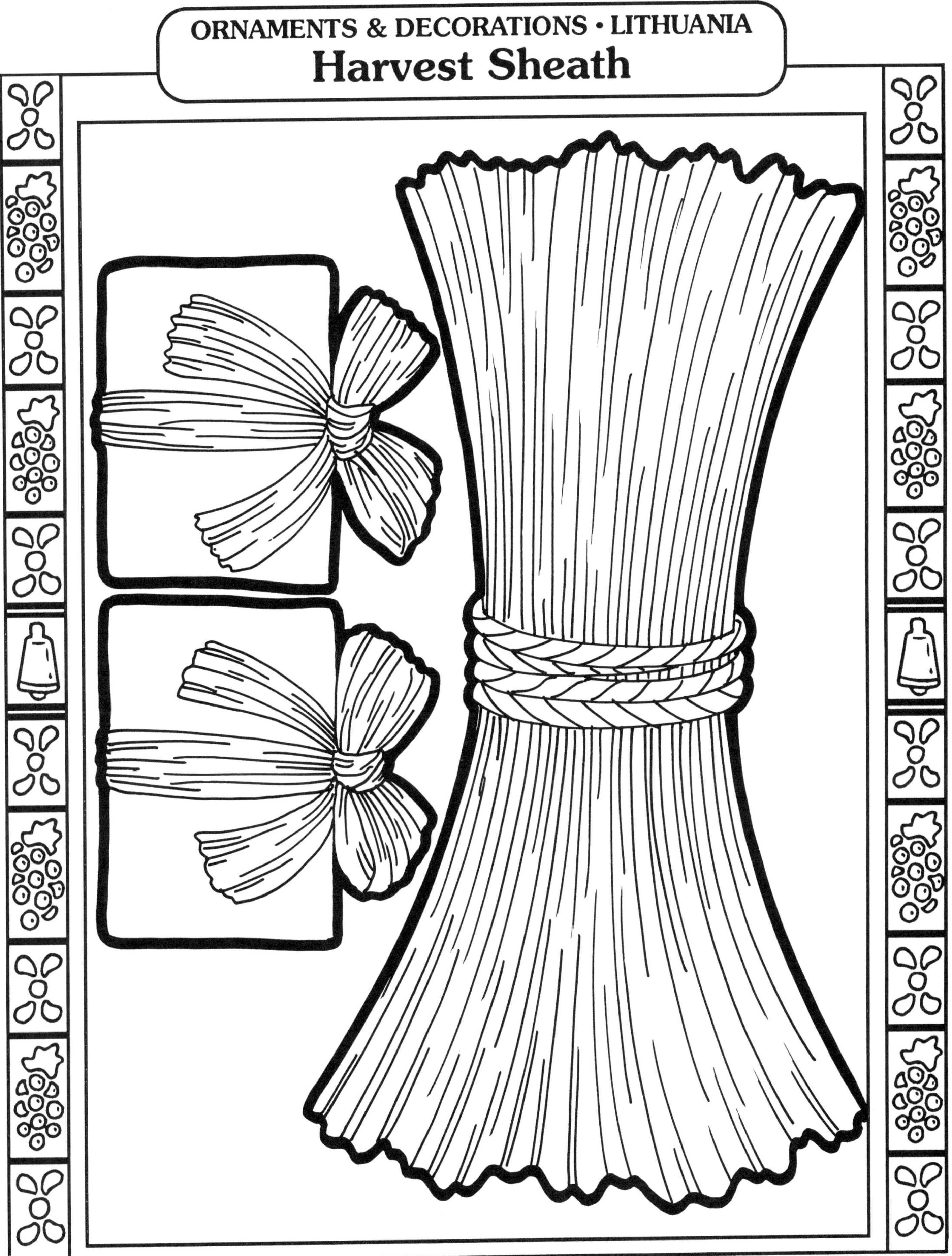

Europe

Norway

A Norwegian legend tells of an invisible group of people who worked through the night to help a farmer harvest his grain fields.

The farmer and his wife were not able to harvest the fields alone and planned to ask their neighbors for help. One evening they prepared food and beverage to share with their neighbors at the end of the harvest. The next morning they discovered that the fields had been harvested and the beverage was gone.

Traditionally, sheaths of harvested grain were stacked in the fields in the shape of a cross. But on this morning the sheaths had been tied in a straight knot. And at the bottom of the beverage barrel they found three silver spoons. In keeping with the legend, silver spoons are handed down from generation to generation.

Poland

Dozynki is a harvest festival celebrated in Poland. At the end of the harvest farm workers gather to participate in a traditional custom known as "the decoration of the quail."

The farm workers gather around a stack of grain left in the field. The grain is fashioned into a tripod made of three braids of grain tied together. Bread, salt, and copper coins are placed on a cloth placed under the tripod on the ground (once symbols of wealth). Then the ground around the tripod is plowed.

After the decoration of the quail, the farm workers sing and dance on their way to the landowner's house. There they present the landowner and his family with wreaths made of grain and wildflowers. The song and dance continue and all share a feast which includes meat, bread, cake, apples, and sweet beverages.

Three Silver Spoons

Share the Norwegian legend of invisible harvest helpers with your class. Then provide each student with spoons reproduced on gray construction or poster paper, crayons, scissors, a hole punch, and festive holiday ribbons to make lovely take-home gifts.

1. Color and cut out the spoons.
2. Punch a hole at the top of each spoon.
3. Lace a length of ribbon through each spoon.
4. Tie a bow at the top.
5. Write a message on the back of each spoon.

Wildflower Wreaths

Have your students make wildflower wreaths for take-home door decorations. Provide students with cutout pictures of wildflowers from old magazines or flower catalogs and the materials listed below.

Materials:
- wildflower cutouts
- wreath pattern
- crayons or markers
- scissors
- glue
- ribbon

1. Color and cut out the wreath.
2 Glue cutout wildflowers around your wreath.
3. Punch a hole at the top of the wreath.
4. Lace and tie a bow of ribbon through the hole.

Europe

Scotland

Parties, games, fortune-telling, ghost stories, bonfires, and pranking are traditional activities on *Halloween* in Scotland. Comical masqueraders perform in old costumes from house to house, then pass a hat for money.

Similar to apple bobbing, a tub is filled with water and apples with one difference. The apples are whirled around in the tub and players try to skewer them with forks dropped from clenched teeth.

Window tapping is a popular and harmless prank. To pull the prank you need two strings, one long and one short. A pin is tied to one end of the long string and the short string is tied to the long string about one inch away from the pin. A button is attached to the loose end of the short string, and then the pin is attached to the wood outside a window. With the loose end of the long string in hand, at a distance from the house, tapping begins. Gently pull the string, then immediately slacken it. Each time this is done the button taps the window. If someone comes to investigate, pull the string hard to release the pin and hide.

Spain

The *Vintage Fiesta*, a grape harvest festival, is celebrated in the town called Jerez de la Frontera. The festival includes a parade of horsemen in costume, flower-filled carriages with girls who wave to the crowds, horse races, music, singing, and dancing.

Vintage Fiesta Carriage

Decorate your classroom with colorful student-made Vintage Fiesta Carriages. Provide students with 2" (5.08 cm) squares of colored craft tissue, a hole punch, crayons or markers, glue, a 9" x 12" (22.86 x 30.48 cm) sheet of construction paper, and the patterns below and on page 113.

1. Color and cut out the patterns.
2. Cut pattern A apart along the bold lines.
3. Punch a hole at each dot of each pattern piece.
4. Twist 2" (5.08 cm) squares of craft tissue to form flowers as shown.
5. Insert the tissue flowers through each hole in the carriage.
6. Assemble and glue the patterns to a sheet of construction paper as shown.
7. Write your name on the carriage.

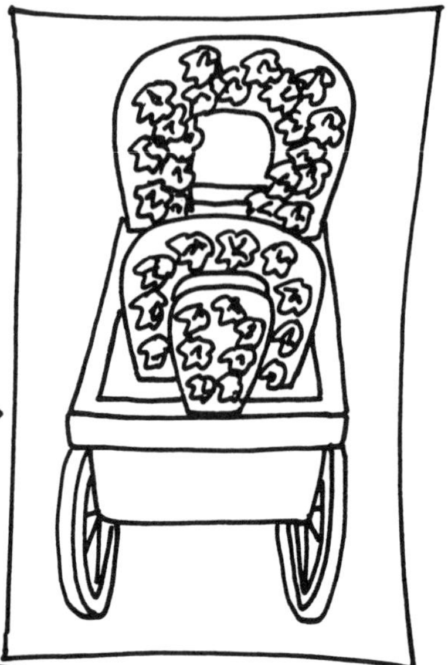

A

Vintage Fiesta Carriage

Sweden

Martinmas

The medieval harvest festival of *Martinmas* is celebrated in Sweden, Germany, the Netherlands, and Switzerland. In Sweden it is called *Marten Gås*, (pronounced mar-ten goohs.) Every November, at the end of the harvest season, farmers would share a feast from their harvest with beggars. Today children dress as beggars and go from house to house carrying lanterns. They sing silly songs and receive goodies such as candy, fruit, and cake.

Gotland Games

The *Gotland Games*, a sports festival, takes place in Gotland, an island off the coast of Sweden. During this festival teams from different villages compete in ten sporting events: wrestling; foot races; *varpa* and *caber*, both hurling contests; and more.

In the game of *Varpa*, the contestants throw six-pound stones or weights at a stake 60 feet (18.2 m) away. Similar to the Olympic event of shot put, the goal is to throw the stone the furthest distance. It's possible this sport was played by the Vikings centuries ago because the stones used in the game have been found in Viking graves.

Hurling the *caber* is similar to throwing a javelin, another Olympic event. However, in this event, the *caber* is a heavy pole the size of a tree trunk. The goal is to throw the *caber* the greatest distance, making sure it turns end over end at least once before landing.

Gotland Games Headdress

Your students will love wearing Viking headdresses when they participate in a game of *Varpa* with beanbags (see page 116). Reproduce and provide each student with the pattern below, crayons or markers, scissors, glue, a stapler, and a 2" x 20" (5.08 x 50.8 cm) oaktag strip to make Viking headbands.

1. Color and cut out the pattern.
2. Glue the pattern to the oaktag strip.
3. Wrap the headband to fit around your head and secure with staples.
4. Write your name inside the headband.

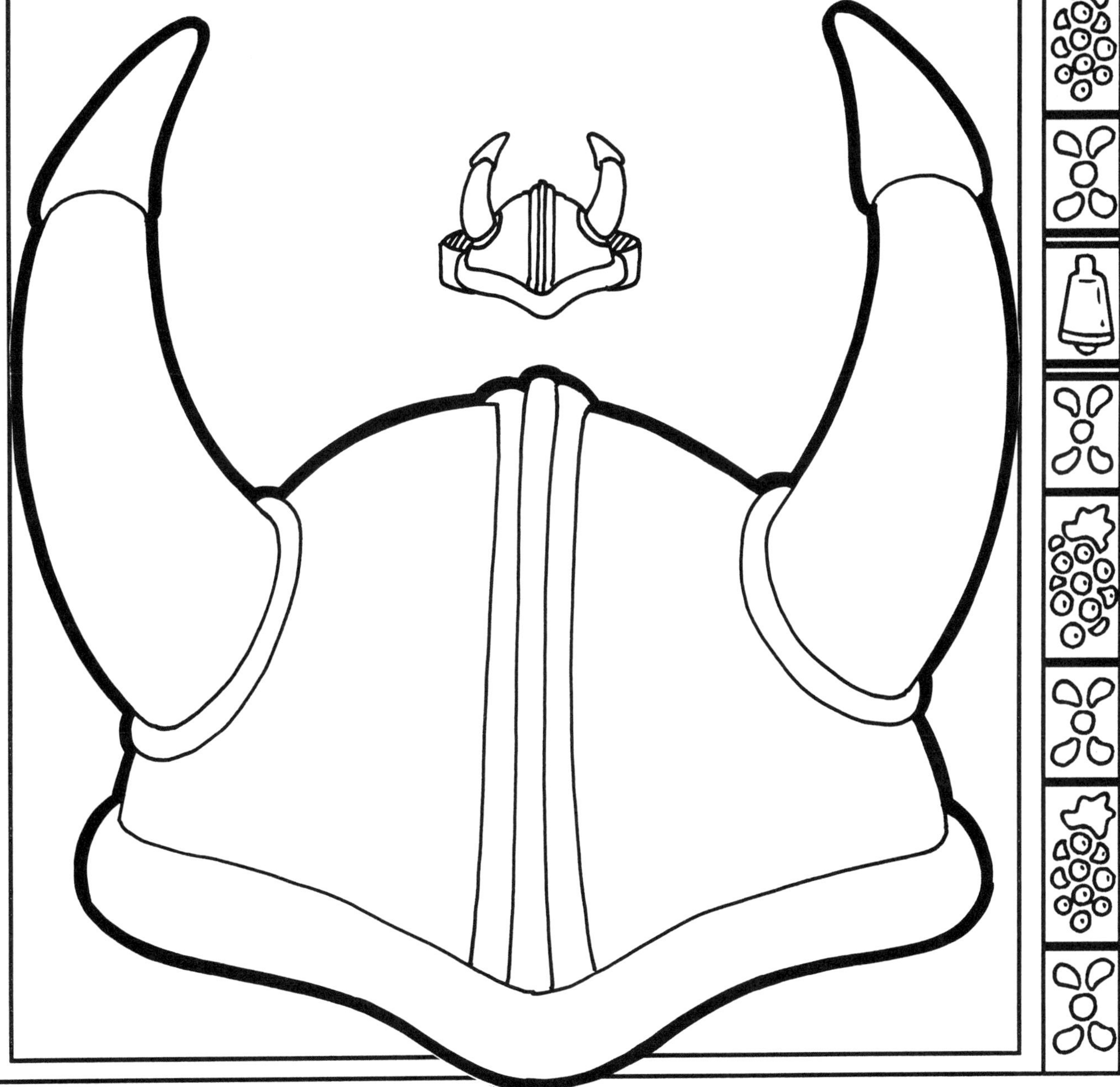

Varpa Beanbag Toss

Make beanbags for students to participate in a game of *Varpa* in celebration of Sweden's Gotland games. Use the take-home note on page 121 asking parent volunteers to help assemble beanbags and provide Gotland Game cupcakes for students to share at the end of the game.

Reproduce the medallion pattern below on yellow, gray, and brown construction paper for gold, silver, and bronze awards. Provide each child with the Gotland Game cupcake topper to color and cut out. Show how to attach a toothpick to the back of cupcake topper with cellophane tape.

Prepare a game arena outside or in an open area of your class. Mark the starting line with masking tape. Use an empty milk container filled with sand as a stake and place it 10-15 feet (3-4.5 m) from the starting line. Draw two columns on a sheet of paper. Write each child's name in the first column. Label the second column "Score." Assign two students to act as game officials to keep score while the game is in play.

To play:

1. In turn, each child, standing upright (no leaning), tosses a beanbag at the stake (milk container) with one hand.
2. One game official marks and measures the distance of the toss.
3. A second game official writes the distance on the score sheet.
4. Award gold, silver, and bronze medallions to the first, second, and third place winners.

Note: Players with identical scores should toss again.
Extend the distance between the starting line and the stake for older students.

Europe

Switzerland

Some European harvest festivals are celebrated in the form of market days like the *Onion Market* which is celebrated in Switzerland. This custom dates back to a time when the city of Bern granted the merchants of Fribourg permission to sell their farm products in Bern's market square. This was a grateful gesture for help received from the Fribourg citizens when the city of Bern was nearly destroyed by fire. The festival gets its name from the fact that Fribourg's only farm product was onions.

Every November the Bern market square is filled with bunches, boxes, and baskets of onions. The people dress in traditional native and onion costumes. They drink onion soup, eat onion salad, and onion cake. And children enjoy eating onion-shaped candies.

Yugoslavia

With autumn comes preparation for winter. A few European countries including certain areas in Yugoslavia practice a traditional custom of using donkeys to carry firewood down from the hills in preparation for the winter months.

Onion Pencil Topper & Name Tag

Celebrate a Swiss Onion Market with your class in November. Provide the pattern below for students to make a pencil topper or name tag. Reproduce additional onions to hang around your classroom.

Materials:

- crayons or markers
- scissors
- a hole punch
- a pencil
- a safety pin
- cellophane tape
- yellow yarn

Pencil Topper

1. Color and cut out the patterns.
2. Punch a hole at each dot on the pencil topper pattern.
3. Thread a pencil through the holes as shown.

Name Tag

1. Write your name on the onion name tag.
2. Attach a safety pin to the back with cellophane tape.

Decorations

1. Punch a hole at the top of several pencil topper patterns.
2. Lace and tie assorted lengths of yellow yarn to the onions.
3. Tie the loose ends of yarn together and hang.

Onion Headdress

Use the take-home note on page 121 to ask parents to prepare onion-shaped sandwiches for your students to share at your Onion Market. Provide 2" x 20" (5.08 x 50.8 cm) strips of green construction paper, scissors, glue, cellophane tape, and onion patterns for students to make Onion Market headbands.

Onion Sandwiches

1. Cut two slices of toast into onion shapes as shown.
2. Prepare the sandwich.
3. Cut and insert green onion stems at the top of the onion sandwich.

Onion Headdress

1. Glue a stem to each onion.
2. Apply glue to the back of each onion and attach it to the green construction paper strip.
3. Wrap the headband around your head to fit and secure with tape.
4. Write your name on the inside of the headband.

Firewood Express

Have children collect small twigs to complete this project. Cover your bulletin board with green paper and attach autumn-colored leaves for the border. Provide each student with a donkey and two basket patterns, two empty milk cartons, and the materials listed below. Reproduce the patterns on poster board. And cut the tops of the milk cartons before distributing to children (see diagram). The completed project can double as a crayon or pencil holder.

Materials:
- crayons or markers
- scissors
- glue

1. Color and cut out the donkey.
2. Apply glue and attach each basket pattern to a milk carton.
3. Attach the milk carton baskets to each side of the donkey.
4. Fill the baskets with twigs.

A TAKE-HOME NOTE FROM
EUROPE

NORTH AMERICA

Canada

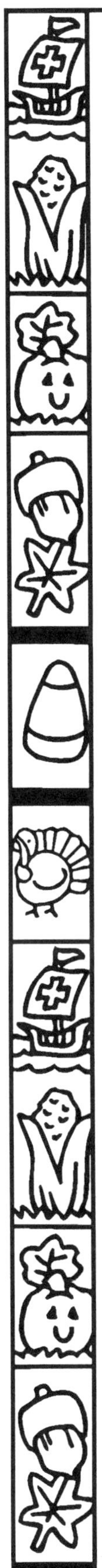

Labor Day

Canadians celebrate *Labor Day* on the first Monday in September to honor their workers. The activities are similar to those of early American Labor Day celebrations.

St. Catherine's Day

St. Catherine's Day or *Santa Catarina* is celebrated on the 25th of November. A seventeenth-century school teacher allowed her students to pull toffee in honor of St. Catherine. As a result, toffee pulling became a traditional custom. See page 152 for more information about St. Catherine and traditional holiday customs that occur during a St. Catherine's Day celebration.

Thanksgiving

Canadians celebrate *Thanksgiving* in much the same manner as the people in the United States; however, there are no parades or spectacular displays associated with this holiday.

The Canadian people give thanks for good things received from the earth as proclaimed in 1879. Traditional customs bring families and friends together to share a meal on the second Monday in October. The first official Canadian Thanksgiving was in 1871.

Toffee Treats

Use the take-home note on page 141 asking for parent volunteers to help assemble Toffee Treats for your students in celebration of St. Catherine's Day.

1. Color and cut out the patterns.
2. Apply glue to the back of the wheel pattern and attach it to the center of the lace circle.
3. Punch a hole in the center of each pattern.
4. Tie a length of yarn around 3 wrapped pieces of toffee.
5. Gather and thread the loose ends of yarn through the hole.
6. Tie the yarn lengths in a knot.

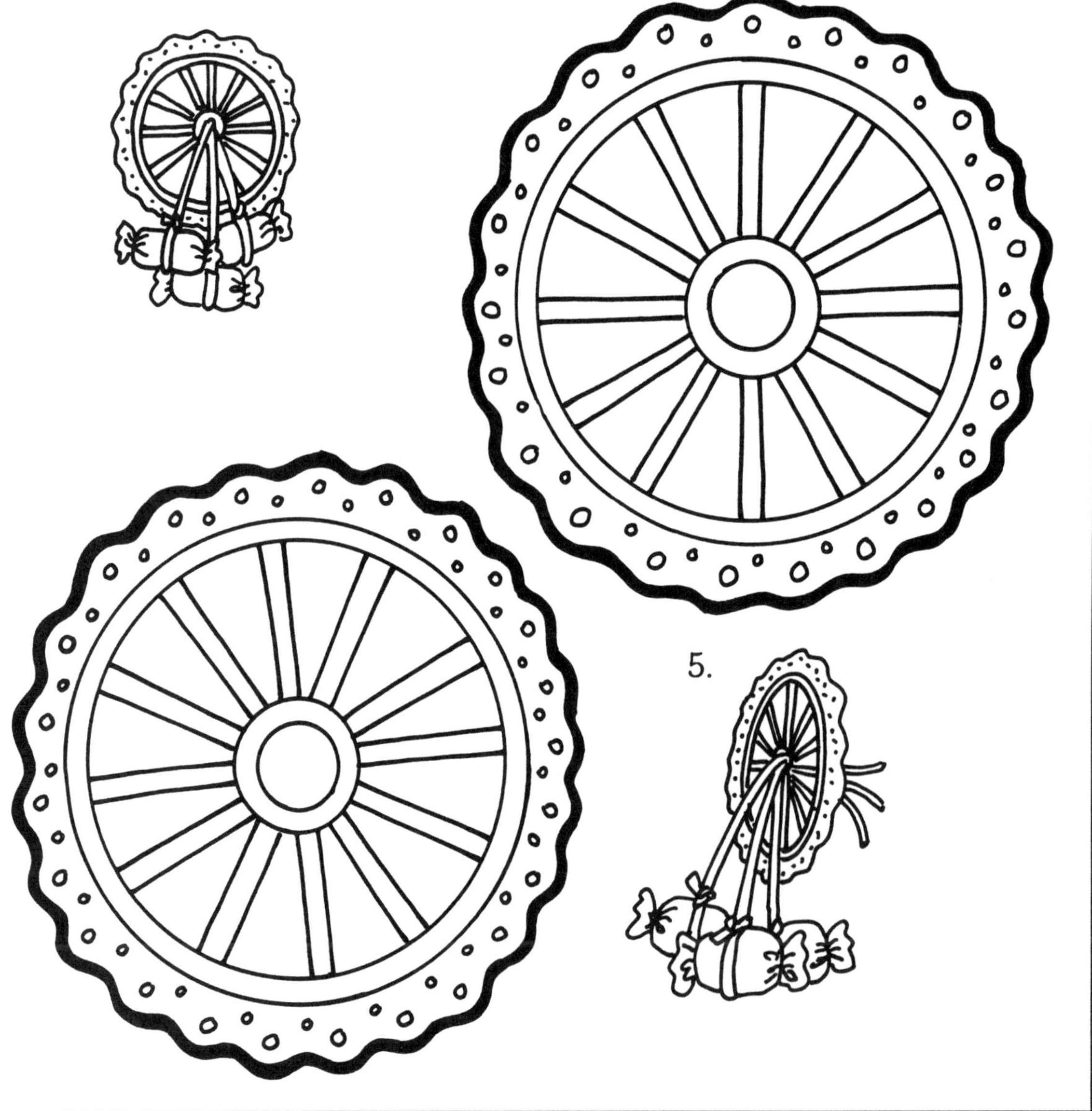

Thanksgiving Collage

Divide students into four groups. Provide each group with a 17" x 24" (43.18 x 60.96 cm) sheet of poster board. Reproduce and provide each group with multiple copies of the patterns below and magazines for cutout pictures to create colorful Thanksgiving collages. Prepare a table with additional supplies such as acorns, crayons or markers, scissors, glue, craft tissue, construction paper, and cotton balls.

North America

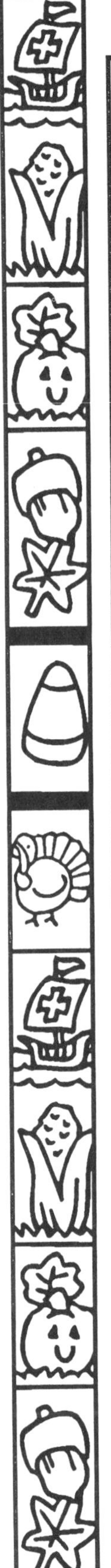

Mexico

Mexicans celebrate their freedom from Spanish rule in September. They gained their independence after a successful revolution against the Spanish colonial government on September 15, 1810.

On October 12, Mexico celebrates the accomplishments of one the world's most famous explorers, Christopher Columbus, and the discovery of America. This day is known as *Día de la Raza* (Day of the Race). The celebration also addresses the common heritage between both Spanish and Indian people of Hispanic nations.

El Dia de los Santos, All Saints' Day, is a widely celebrated feast in Mexico. This feast occurs on the second day of November.

A few days before Halloween, youngsters sell wood to make money for purchases of fruit, candies, and cookies. These treats are then placed in large wicker baskets carried by burros. On the eve of El Dia de los Santos, November 1, each household prepares a meal and a special table with a place setting in honor of each departed family member. The place settings consist of a dish of food, a lighted candle, a bouquet of flowers, and treats from the wicker baskets. At the end of the day families share the treats from the table.

The next morning, November 2, families visit cemeteries to tidy graves and replace faded flowers with new ones.

Halloween Burro Baskets

Use the take-home note on page 141 asking parents to send Halloween treats to fill student-made burro baskets. Provide each child with the patterns below, crayons or markers, scissors, glue, and a 12" x 18" (30.48 x 45.72 cm) sheet of construction paper. Display completed projects on a bulletin board covered with orange poster paper and green borders.

1. Color and cut out the patterns.
2. Fold the tabs on each basket along the dotted lines.
3. Apply glue to the back of the burro and attach it to the sheet of construction paper.
4. Apply glue to the tabs on each basket and attach one to each side of the burro.
5. Fill your burro baskets with Halloween treats.

United States

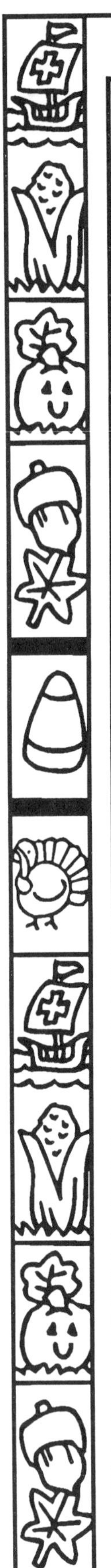

Autumn Aloft

Park City, Utah, attracts hundreds of hot-air balloon pilots for its annual *Hot-Air Balloon Festival* held in September.

Alaska Day

On October 18, 1867, the United States flag replaced the Russian flag over Sitka. This ceremony formally transferred the ownership of Alaska to the United States.

Black Poetry Day

Jupiter Hammond, born in New York on October 17, 1711, was the first African American to publish his own verse. Today we honor Mr. Hammond and recognize contributions made by African American poets on the anniversary of his birthday. The African American Poetry Day Committee is located in Plattsburgh, New York.

Discoverer's Day

Hawaiians celebrate *Discoverer's Day* on the second Monday in October. The celebration honors all discoverers.

Discovery Day

The Island of Puerto Rico, a Commonwealth of the United States, celebrates *Discovery Day* on November 19. This public holiday is observed in honor of the discovery of Puerto Rico by Christopher Columbus on his second voyage to the New World in 1493. In the sixteenth century the island was known as *Borinquen*; today, its official name is *Estado Libre Asociado de Puerto Rico*.

Balloon Bonanza

Celebrate an Autumn Aloft festival with your class. Help students assemble hot-air balloons to decorate the classroom.

Materials:
- crayons or markers
- scissors
- a hole punch
- two 6" (15.24 cm) lengths of yarn
- glue

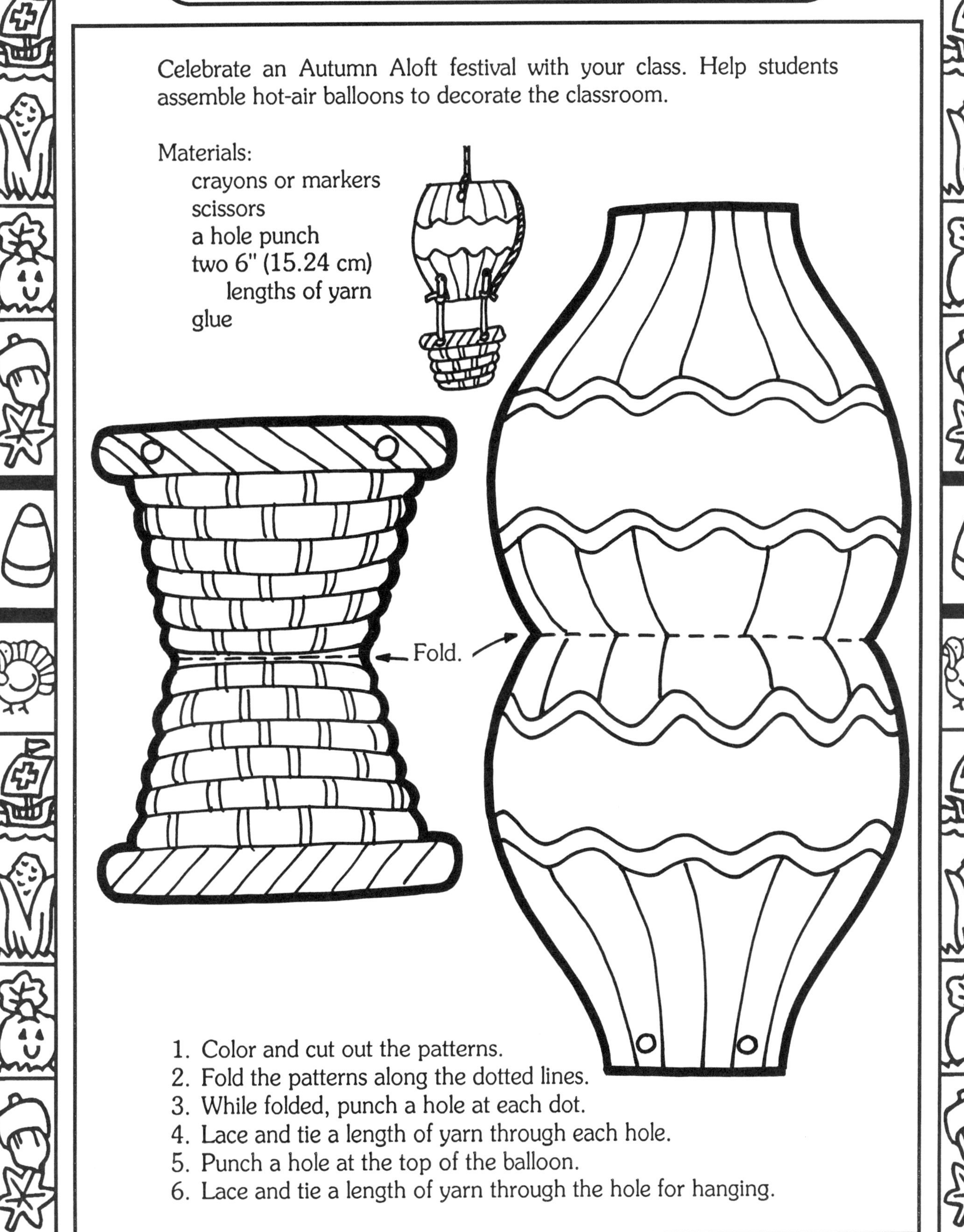

1. Color and cut out the patterns.
2. Fold the patterns along the dotted lines.
3. While folded, punch a hole at each dot.
4. Lace and tie a length of yarn through each hole.
5. Punch a hole at the top of the balloon.
6. Lace and tie a length of yarn through the hole for hanging.

Flags over Sitka

Enlarge the pattern of Alaska below to fit in the center of your bulletin board. Cover the bulletin board with light blue paper and white border strips. Reproduce a United States flag (page 184) for each student in your class. Provide students with red and blue crayons or markers. Show students how to attach flags to plastic straws. Display completed flags in an arc above the map of Alaska.

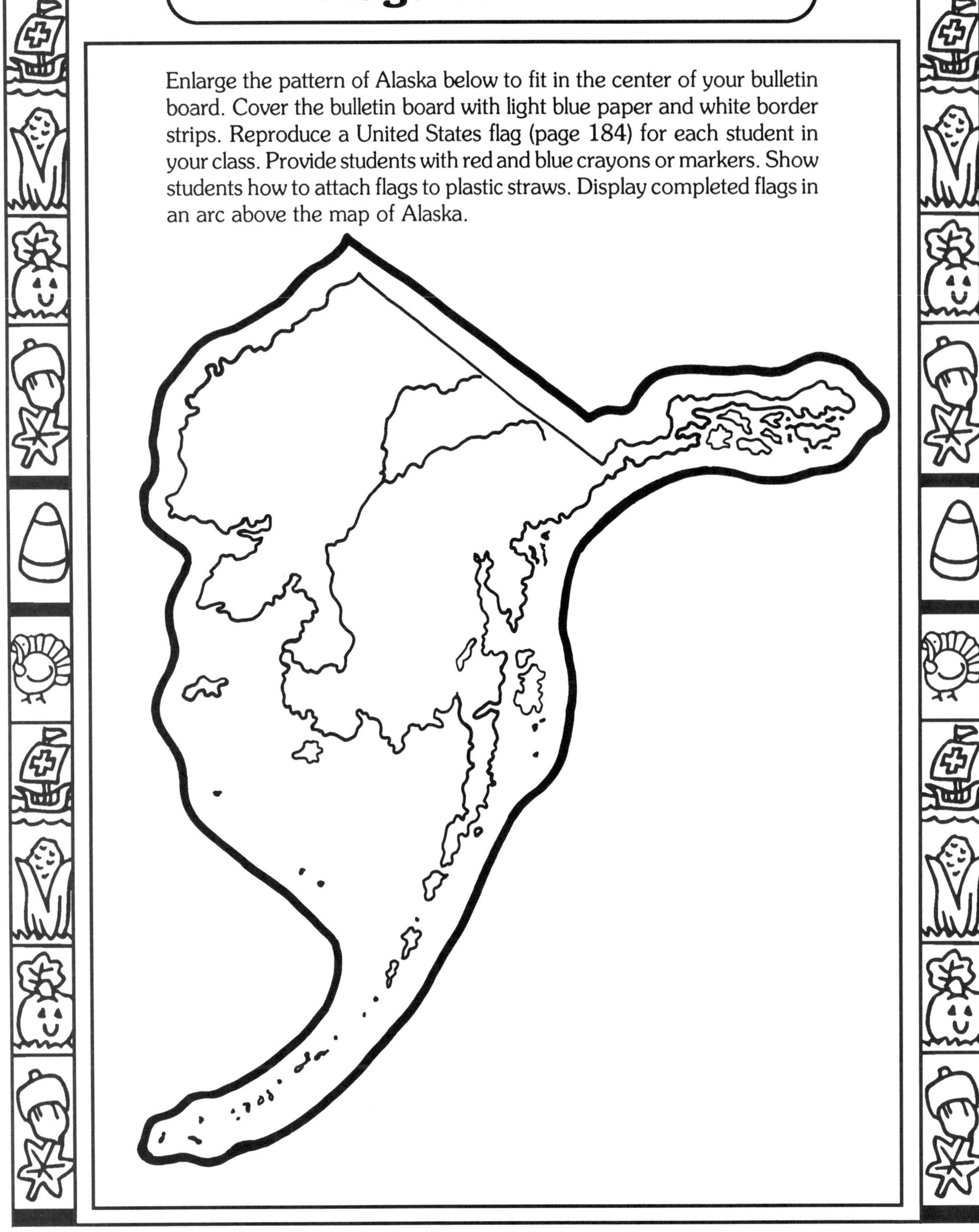

Poetry Panorama

Prepare a unit on African-American poetry to share with your class. Then ask students to write poems that reflect what they learned. Provide students with the pattern below for students to write final drafts of their poems. Mount poems on classroom walls in a continuous panorama.

Happy Birthday, Borinquen!

Provide each child in your class with the pattern and materials listed below to create a Happy Birthday, Borinquen! bulletin board display. Cover your bulletin board with red poster paper and blue border strips. Enlarge and color the banner for your bulletin board title.

Materials:
- crayons or markers
- scissors
- glue
- 9" x 12" (22.86 x 30.48 cm) white construction paper

1. Color and cut out the patterns.
2. Assemble and glue the patterns to a sheet of construction paper.
3. Write your name at the bottom of the picture.

Feast of San Gennaro

Every year, for eleven days in September, people crowd the streets of Little Italy in New York City to celebrate the *Feast of San Gennaro*.

San Gennaro or St. Januarius is honored as the protector (patron saint) of Naples, Italy. In the year 305 he suffered death by sword. Before he died he convinced many people who treated him unjustly to change their religious beliefs.

Today the anniversary of his death is celebrated in New York City on the half-mile stretch of Mulberry Street. The street is filled with music, laughter, and every variety of Italian foods such as sausages, peppers, clams, calzones, and more. The festival begins each morning around 9 and continues to midnight.

A San Gennaro Festival

Have your class participate in a mini festival celebrating the Feast of San Gennaro. Use the take-home note on page 141 to ask each parent to send soft drinks, cupcakes, or finger sandwiches for student-manned festival booths. Provide children with red, green, and white construction paper and crepe paper streamers to decorate their desks as festival booths. Reproduce the Italian flag on page 172 and the banner below for students to make San Gennaro Festival banners.

1. Color and cut out the banner.
2. Glue the flag to the banner.
3. Attach the banner and flag to the front of your desk.

Fire Prevention Week

Every year since 1925, by Presidential Proclamation, one week in October is observed as Fire Prevention Week. The events of the week are dedicated to increasing the public's awareness of the dangers of fire and fire safety.

United States

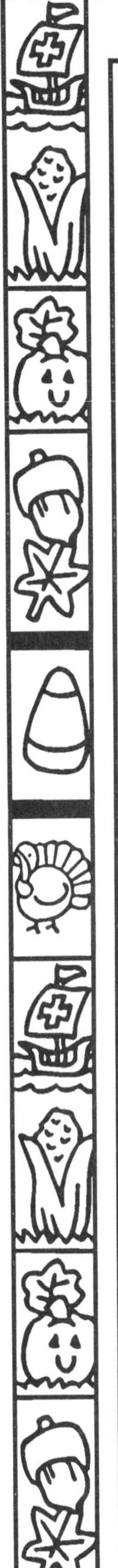

Halloween

Halloween is a nighttime fall festival enthusiastically celebrated by children of all ages in the United States. Children dress in a variety of costumes and go from house to house asking for treats. This is known as trick-or-treating. Traditional costumes include white-sheet ghosts, witches draped in black, and scary monsters. Today children dress as clowns, ballerinas, soldiers, pumpkins, martians, playful dinosaurs, colorful cartoon and comic characters, and more. Adults enjoy the festivities as well with elaborate costume parties, and on occasion parents dress up to greet trick-or-treaters at the door.

Popular treats include candy corn, lollipops, and individually wrapped candy bars. Occasionally stickers, bookmarks, pencils, and other small toy items can be found in a trick-or-treater's treasure bag.

Even the bags carried by children on Halloween night come in all shapes and sizes. Paper bags, pillowcases, plastic jack-o'-lanterns, and ghost-shaped containers are used to collect the delicious variety of treats given on this night.

Halloween is observed on October 31. In most states trick-or-treat activities begin at dusk and last for two to three hours. In some communities, schools, churches, and businesses provide safe Halloween activities for children—bazaars, haunted castles, and game rooms to name a few.

Regardless of the location, no rain, nor sleet, nor hail could stop loyal, costume-clad trick-or-treaters from parading through neighborhood streets on Halloween night.

Halloween Hoedown

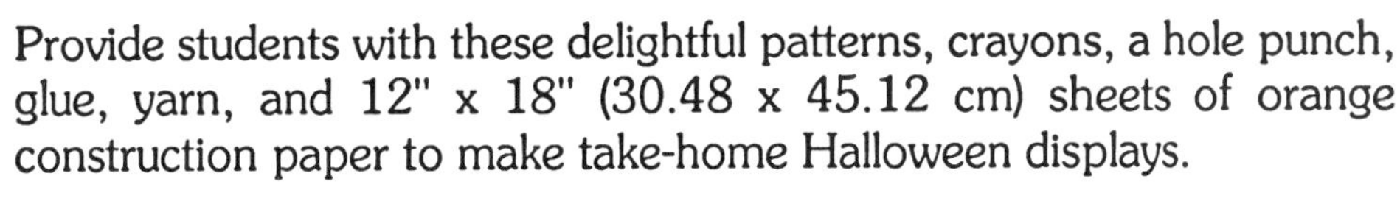

Provide students with these delightful patterns, crayons, a hole punch, glue, yarn, and 12" x 18" (30.48 x 45.12 cm) sheets of orange construction paper to make take-home Halloween displays.

1. Color and cut out the patterns.
2. Assemble and glue the patterns to a sheet of construction paper.
3. Punch a hole at each top corner of your picture.
4. Lace and tie a length of yarn through each hole for hanging.

United States

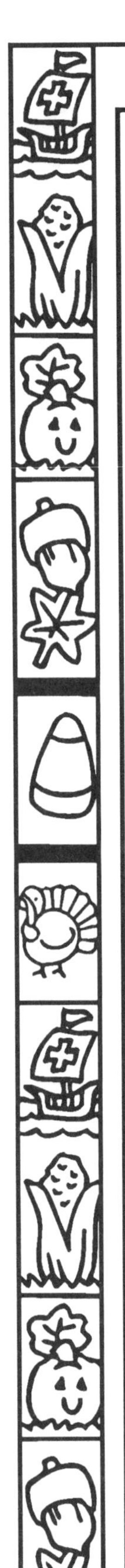

Johnny Appleseed Day

Johnny Appleseed, born John Chapman, was an American frontier hero. He is well known for planting orchards throughout Pennsylvania and Illinois. Johnny Appleseed wore a tin pan for a hat and walked barefoot. Americans celebrate the anniversary of his birthday on September 26.

Apple Harvest Jubilee

Celebrate Johnny Appleseed's birthday with your class. Serve apple juice, applesauce, apple pie, and apple butter sandwiches provided by parent volunteers. Provide students with red construction paper apples to write birthday greetings to Johnny Appleseed. Cut simple basket shapes from brown grocery bags. Mount baskets on a bulletin board entitled Apple Harvest Jubilee. Have students attach apple greetings to the baskets.

Labor Day

Labor Day is celebrated in many countries around the world in honor of each nation's working people. The United States and Canada Labor Day occurs on the first Monday in September.

In 1882, Peter McGuire, a leader in the labor community, initiated steps to make a special day for all American workers. Labor leaders agreed, resulting in the first American Labor Day Parade on September 5, 1882, in New York. After the parade there were speeches followed by fireworks and a picnic.

Prior to this date, Labor Day was reserved for the laboring class which included mostly factory workers. The parade was successful and continued as an annual celebration.

In 1887, a few states adopted Labor Day as a holiday and in 1894, the President proclaimed Labor Day a legal holiday.

Thousands of workers marched in the first parade and over a hundred thousand marched in the 1959 Labor Day parade in New York City. The parades gave workers an opportunity to voice their concerns about working conditions and unfair practices in the workplace. Marchers carried signs describing working conditions and quotes from the Constitution. Although parades are no longer common events, many workers have the day off, which was one of the primary goals of Mr. McGuire.

Provide students with butcher paper, old magazines for cutout pictures, and a variety of craft supplies to create Labor Day banners. Encourage children to write slogans referring to different occupations.

United States

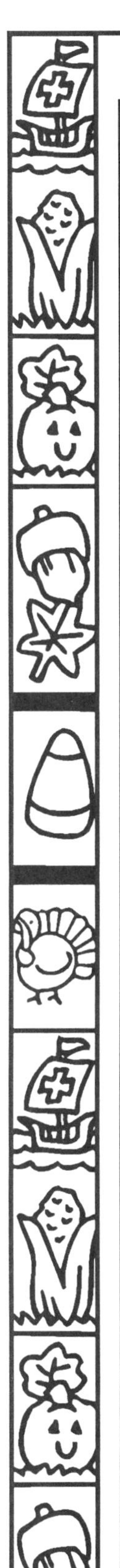

National Grandparents Day

National Grandparents Day is celebrated on the first Sunday after Labor Day in September in honor of all grandparents. This day is assigned to giving grandparents an opportunity to share their affection with their children and grandchildren, and increase children's awareness of the guidance older people can offer.

Pumpkin Festival

The city of Edmonton, Kentucky, celebrates the *Pumpkin Festival* in the month of October. Contests for the largest pumpkin, the best pumpkin pie, arts and crafts displays, and foot races are features of the day.

Oyster Day

Chincoteague Island in Virginia celebrates its annual *Oyster Festival* on the Saturday in October which coincides with Columbus Day. On this day a variety of oyster dishes are served. All-you-can-eat steamed, fried, and stewed oysters are enjoyed by everyone.

Sadie Hawkins Day

Cartoonist Al Capp introduced a day when girls asked boys for a date in the comic strip "Li'l Abner" in the 1930s. Traditionally it was the other way around; boys asked girls for dates. Today the first Saturday in November, and occasionally other days throughout the year, girls take the initiative to ask boys for a date or to dance at a party.

Sandwich Day

Sandwich Day, November 3, honors the Fourth Earl of Sandwich, John Montague, for his practical invention of the sandwich. One night, during an all-night card game, the Earl asked for two slices of bread with a piece of roasted meat between them. Today people all over the world enjoy a variety of sandwich delights from peanut butter and bananas to multi-layered sandwiches known as "Dagwood sandwiches."

Statue of Liberty Day

"Give me your tired, your poor, your huddled masses . . . ," these words are found inside the pedestal of the Statue of Liberty. Ground was broken on Bedloe's Island in New York Harbor in the spring of 1883. Three and a half years later, Frederic Auguste Bartholdi completed the Statue of Liberty. A gift from the French government to the United States, "Lady Liberty" was dedicated on October 28, 1886.

Autumn Greetings

Provide each student in your class with one of the greeting card designs below, a 6" x 12" (15.24 x 30.48 cm) sheet of construction paper, crayons, scissors, and glue to make autumn greeting cards. Instruct children to fold construction paper sheets in half and glue card designs to the front of the cards. Have children write messages in the cards to post on an Autumn Greetings bulletin board.

United States

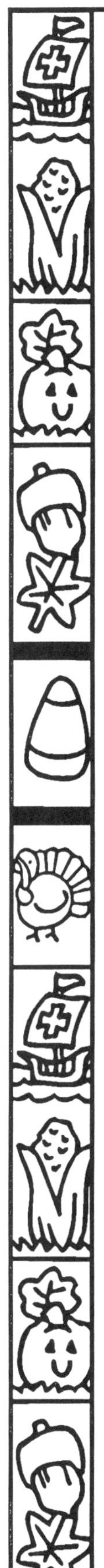

Thanksgiving

In the United States, Thanksgiving is traditionally celebrated in honor of the first settlers of Plymouth, Massachusetts.

Nineteen families set sail on the Mayflower from England to the New World in search of religious freedom. They had a long and difficult journey and struggled to survive in the untamed wilderness. With the help of the native Americans, the Wampanoags, these settlers learned how to survive.

In 1621 the settlers celebrated the first Thanksgiving with their Native American friends. The celebration lasted a few days. Meals included wild game and crops harvested with the help of the Native Americans.

Few Thanksgiving festivals were held throughout America over the following one hundred and fifty years. It wasn't until 1863 that Thanksgiving was proclaimed a national holiday by President Lincoln.

Today, many families gather on Thanksgiving day to share a meal of turkey, cranberry jelly, sweet potatoes, and pumpkin pie. Sporting events, such as football, have also become a tradition in many American households.

Universal Children's Day

The United Nations designated the first Monday in October as Universal Children's Day. This day is observed in more than 120 nations around the world. Activities include festivals and special ceremonies honoring children. Universal Children's Day was first observed in 1953.

Enlarge and reproduce ship patterns for students to color and cut out. Write each student's name on the pennant flag and display on a bulletin board entitled Quest for Freedom.

International Paper Doll Garland

Provide students with crayons, markers, scissors, a variety of craft supplies, and the pattern below for students to make assorted colored construction paper doll garlands. Display pictures of multicultural children dressed in their native attire for students to use as reference when they are decorating their paper doll garlands. Attach garlands across your bulletin board entitled We Celebrate International Children's Day.

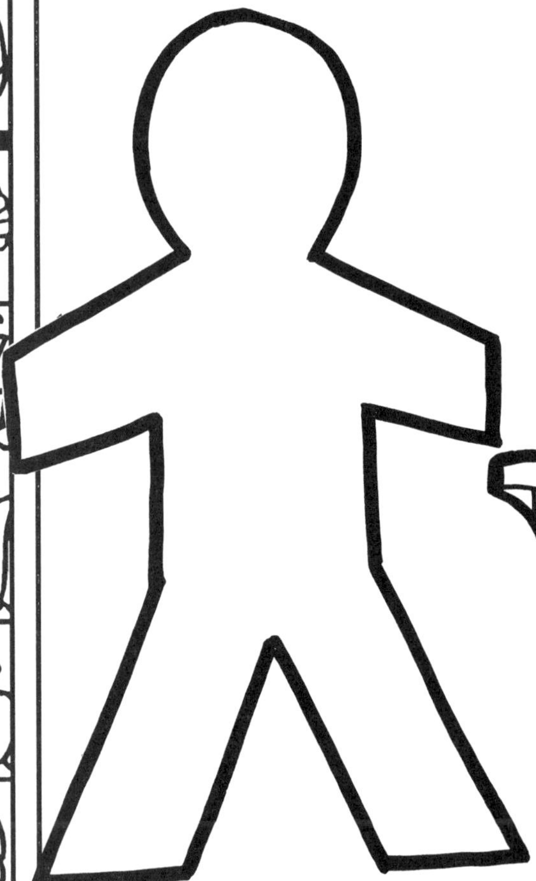

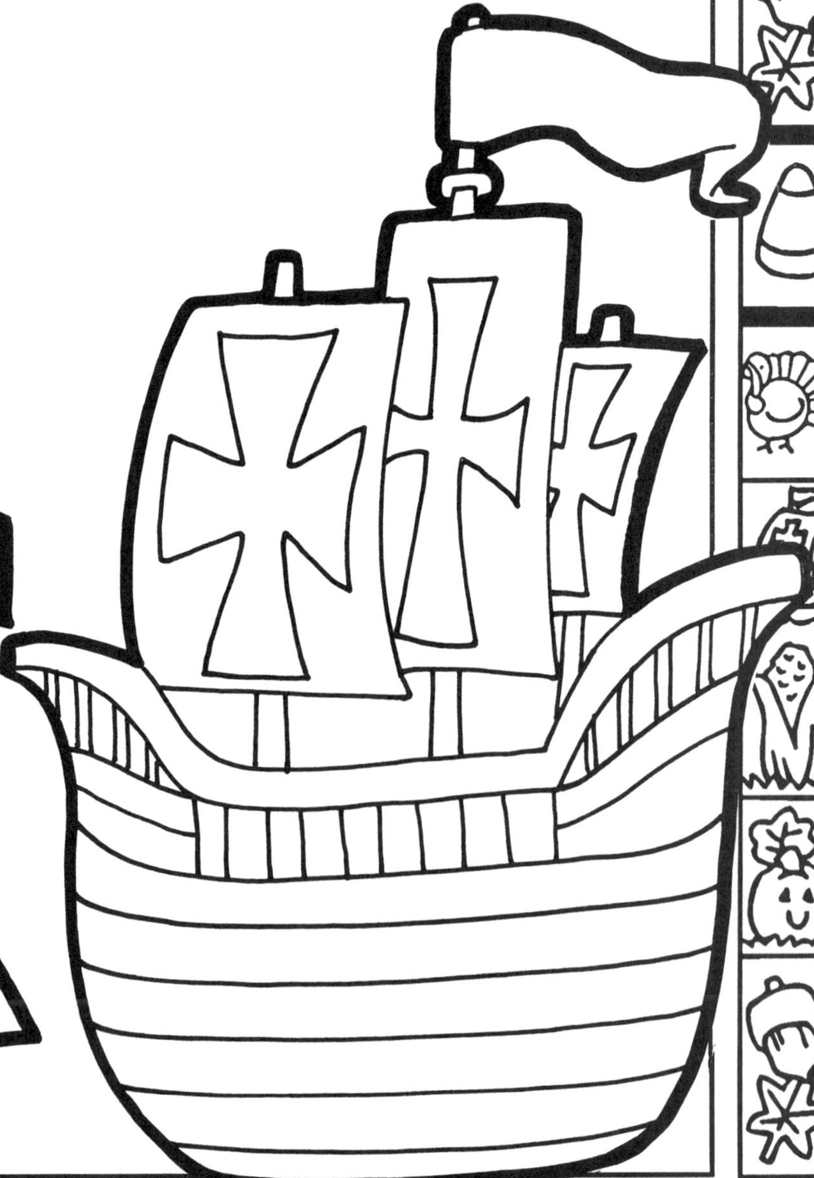

A TAKE-HOME NOTE FROM

NORTH AMERICA

____
Date

Dear _______________________,

We are _______________________

_______________________.

Please _______________________

____

____

____

____

____

____

____

____

____

____

Thank you!

____
Teacher

SOUTH AMERICA

South America

Bolivia

Bolivians celebrate *St. Michael's Day* in September. Dancing is a major activity during the festival. After a brief religious ceremony, dancers in festive costumes dance together in a huge square. Although they dance at the same time, the dancers are not dancing as one group, rather as separate groups in the same square. Between dance performances the groups share meals with family and friends, at the same time but still apart. The activities of this festival illustrate both the distinct boundaries between the separate groups as well as the bridges across the boundaries created in the dance.

Brazil

Brazilians celebrate their freedom from Portuguese rule in September. They gained their independence from Portugal on September 7, 1822.

Colombia

On November 2 in Colombia, children carry a giant cross covered with flowers from door to door. This day is called *Día de los Angelitos* (Day of the Little Angels), also known as All Souls' Day.

A young boy leads the procession of children ringing a bell. The children recite a rhyme as they travel from house to house and receive treats from households they visit which they later share with their families.

Peru

La Fiesta de Agua occurs on the first Sunday in October in Peru. After weeks of restoration to irrigation ditches throughout the countryside, a skyrocket signals the opening of the waters. The waters come from the river Carhuayumac and are allowed to run freely through the ditches until they reach the town of San Pedro de Casta.

The celebration begins with a traditional ceremony performed at the opening of the river, asking for plenty of water for the community. Once this is done a procession travels with the flow of the river into the town.

Little Angel Carton Wrapper

Use the take-home note on page 145 to ask for parent volunteers to help children assemble their Little Angel cartons and provide treats to fill the cartons. Provide each child with a clean milk container, the pattern below, crayons, scissors, cellophane tape, and a 3" x 13" (7.62 x 33.02 cm) strip of colored construction paper. Cut the tops of milk cartons as shown before distributing to children.

1. Color and cut out the pattern.
2. Apply glue to the back of the pattern and attach to the construction paper strip.
3. Wrap the construction paper around a carton, aligning the angel on one side.
4. Fill your Little Angel carton with treats and present it to someone special. Or use it to store crayons, markers, or pencils.

A TAKE-HOME NOTE FROM
SOUTH AMERICA

____
Date

Dear ______________________,

We are ______________________
______________________.

Please ______________________
____
____
____
____
____
____
____
____
____

Thank you!

____
Teacher

Columbus Day

In 1492, Christopher Columbus (in Spanish, Cristóbal Colón) sailed under the Spanish flag to discover the New World.

Columbus, an Italian explorer, born Cristoforo Colombo, met with King Ferdinand and Queen Isabella of Spain who helped to finance an ocean voyage to find a new route to the East Indies. With their help he began his voyage with the promise to claim new lands for Spain. In return, Columbus would receive a small part of the riches and the title of "Admiral of All the Ocean Seas."

Columbus completed his first voyage and returned to Spain with great news of his discoveries and made three more voyages to the New World. Although Columbus never reached the Indies and died without knowledge of the importance of his accomplishments, the world salutes his adventurous spirit and celebrates his voyage of discovery.

President Franklin D. Roosevelt proclaimed October 12 as Columbus Day, a national holiday, in 1937.

Prior to 1937, the earliest known celebrations in honor of Columbus' accomplishments were in New York City and Baltimore, Maryland, in 1792, three hundred years after his discovery of the New World. Three additional celebrations followed over one hundred years later: one in 1905 in Colorado; another in 1906 in Chicago, Illinois; and the third in 1909 in New York State. Earlier celebrations were called Discovery Day. Today it is known as Columbus Day and celebrated as an annual holiday in many North and South American countries and the European countries of Italy and Spain.

Share facts about Columbus and his voyage of discovery with your students. Reproduce the patterns on pages 147-148 for Columbus' Voyage of Discovery classroom display.

Ship Pockets

Create a bulletin board display in honor of Columbus' discovery with student-made ship pockets and the map on page 148. Enlarge the map to fit in the center of your bulletin board and add blue border strips. Provide students with paper plate halves, 2 plastic straws, crayons or markers, scissors, and a stapler to complete this project. Display finished projects on the bulletin board. Store student work, assignments, or fill pockets with treats.

1. Color and cut out the patterns.
2. Attach each sail to a plastic straw.
3. Position and staple each sail to the inside of a paper plate half as shown.
4. Write your name on the ship.
5. Apply glue to back of the ship pattern and attach it to the bottom of a paper plate half.
6. Staple the paper plates together as shown.

A Voyage of Discovery

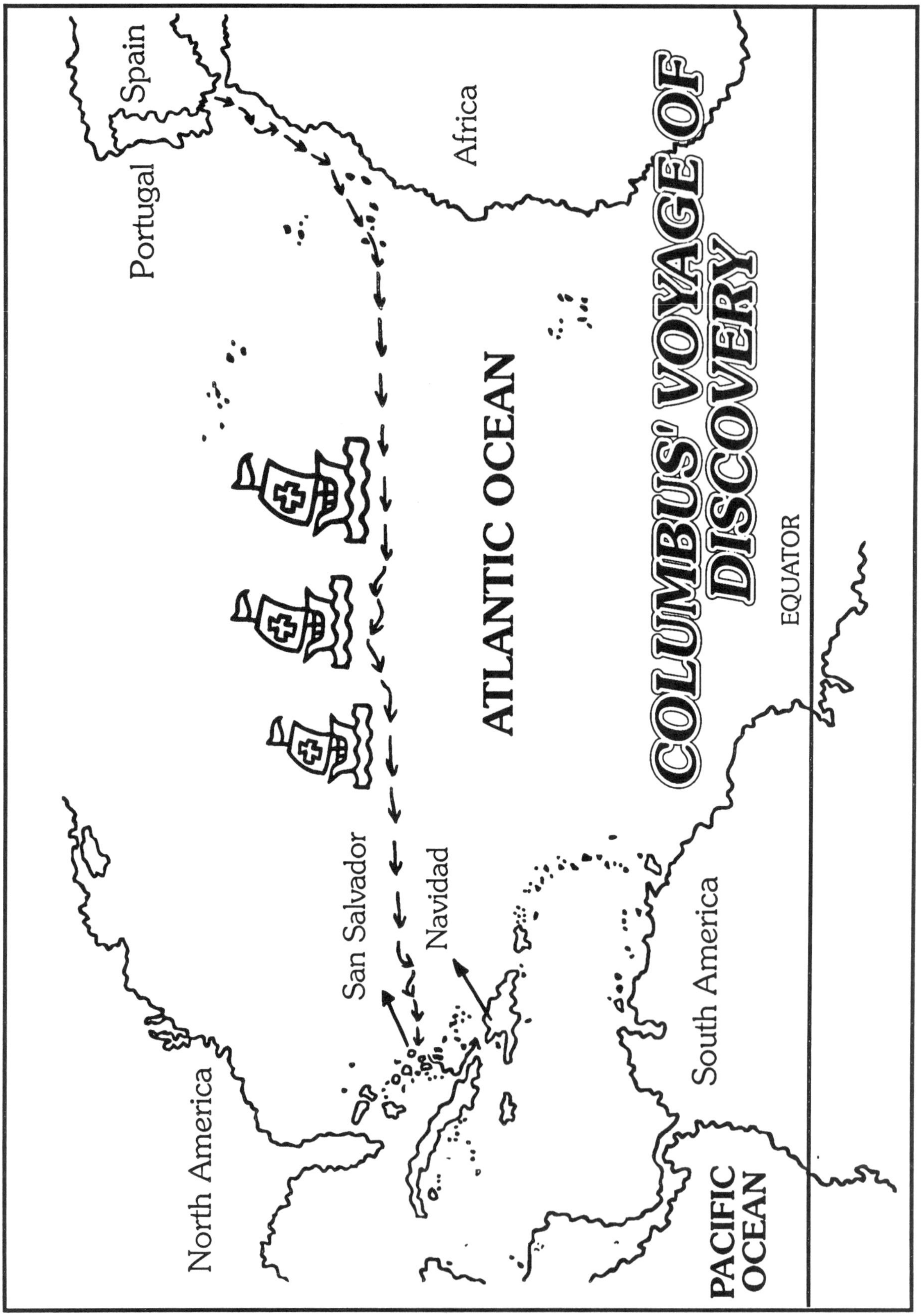

COLUMBUS' VOYAGE OF DISCOVERY

Spain

Portugal

Africa

ATLANTIC OCEAN

EQUATOR

San Salvador

Navidad

North America

South America

PACIFIC OCEAN

Halloween

Halloween, Hallow E'en, or All Hallow's Eve is a nighttime fall festival celebrated primarily by children on October 31. Children dress in a variety of costumes and go from house to house asking for treats, known as trick-or-treating. Traditionally costumes have included white sheet ghosts, witches draped in black, and numerous scary monsters. Today the parade of costumes worn during this night includes a wide variety of scary and humorous characters, both store bought and homemade, which adds to the fun and frolic.

The end of October, according to the ancient Celtic calendar, was the end of the old year, and the last day of the month was considered New Year's Eve. This day was also thought to be the last day of summer, a perfect time for one last celebration with food and games. Halloween is also associated with ancient religious festivals as it is the day before the religious holiday All Saints' Day.

Halloween was once filled with superstition. Activities included fortune-telling as well as activities believed to prevent or promote future events. Apple peelings and nuts were used to foretell the future and young girls would look into mirrors to see their future.

Masks are an important part of the Halloween costume. It was once believed if a person wore a mask on All Hallow's Eve that lurking goblins would not be able to recognize or harm them. Today a variety of masks are worn to complete festival participants' costumes.

Papier-Mâché Jack-o'-Lantern

Have children bring small, brown trash bags and old newspapers to school to complete this project. Cover a table with newspapers, and prepare a solution of 1 part water and 1 part glue for students to assemble their jack-o'-lanterns.

Have students fill their trash bags with crumpled newspapers and tie the bags closed with a length of yarn. Show how to form the bags into pumpkin forms and how to twist the top of the bag into a stem.

Demonstrate how to tear, dip, and wrap three layers of newspaper strips around the stuffed trash bag forms. Allow to dry between layers. Provide orange, green, and black paint, and brushes for students to decorate their jack-o'-lanterns.

Rosh Hashanah

The sounds from the *shofar*, a wind instrument made from a ram's horn, signal the beginning of the Jewish New Year, *Rosh Hashanah*.

It is celebrated on the first two days of the Hebrew month of *Tishri* (September-October) and is the first of the High Holidays observed during the autumn season.

The first day of Rosh Hashanah honors the time when all men are judged for their actions during the past year. Sometimes children sing "Happy Birthday" to the world in honor of the Jewish legend which tells that the world was created on the first day of Tishri. And many families have accepted the modern custom of sending *Shanah Tovah* (good year) greeting cards.

Families gather to share a special meal which includes *challah*, a sweet holiday bread, or slices of apples dipped in honey which represent sweetness and good health for the coming new year. No sour fruits are served. *Challah* is often round. Sometimes it is shaped into a braid or ladder and decorated with birds and ladders.

During the two-day celebration families attend religious services. Each person carefully considers his or her actions during the past year and promises are made to live a better life in the new year.

AROUND THE WORLD • ROSH HASHANAH

Apples, Birds, & Braids

Provide students with the patterns below, a paper plate, crayons or markers, scissors, glue, and a variety of craft supplies to make take-home displays for Rosh Hashanah.

St. Catherine's Day

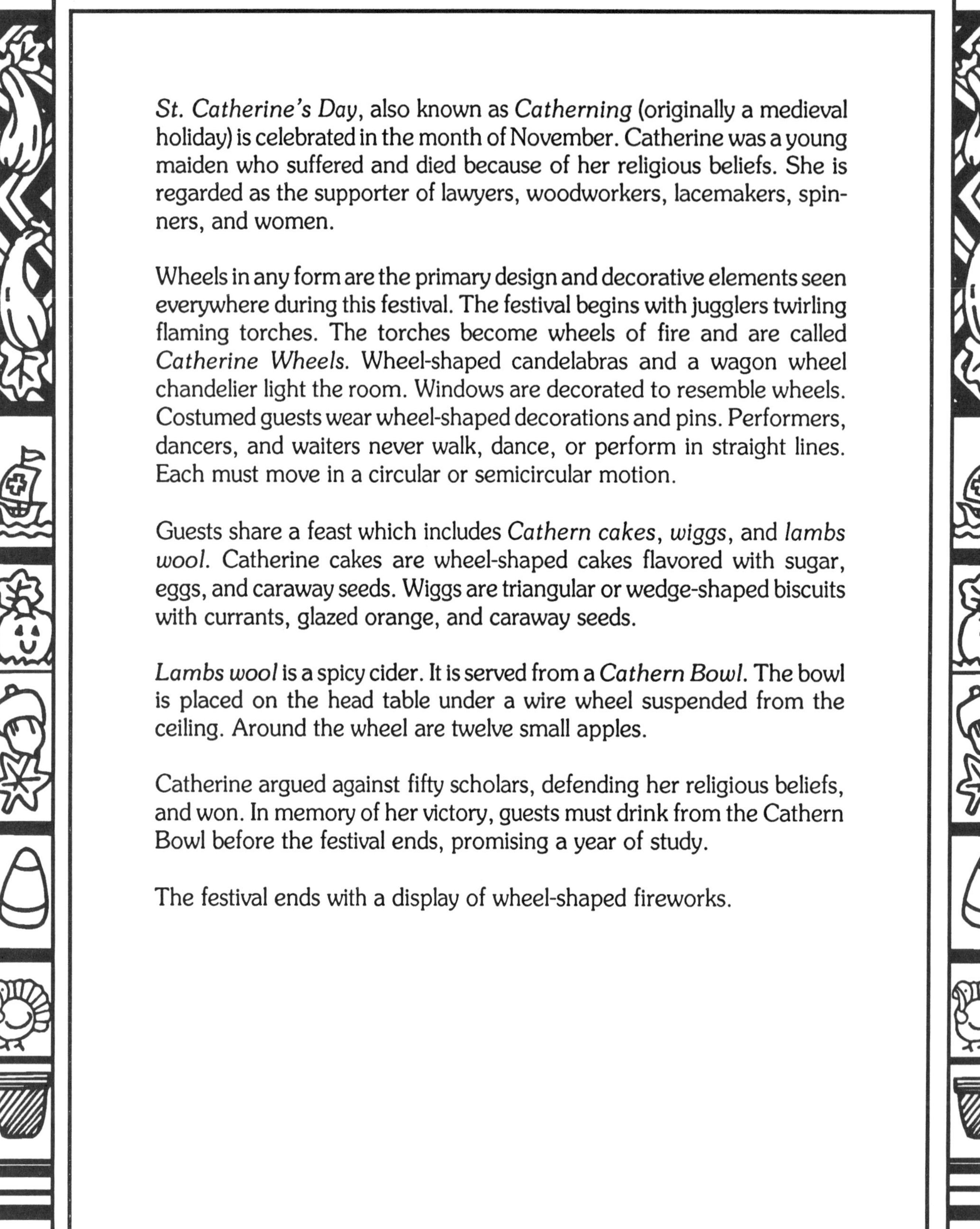

St. Catherine's Day, also known as *Catherning* (originally a medieval holiday) is celebrated in the month of November. Catherine was a young maiden who suffered and died because of her religious beliefs. She is regarded as the supporter of lawyers, woodworkers, lacemakers, spinners, and women.

Wheels in any form are the primary design and decorative elements seen everywhere during this festival. The festival begins with jugglers twirling flaming torches. The torches become wheels of fire and are called *Catherine Wheels.* Wheel-shaped candelabras and a wagon wheel chandelier light the room. Windows are decorated to resemble wheels. Costumed guests wear wheel-shaped decorations and pins. Performers, dancers, and waiters never walk, dance, or perform in straight lines. Each must move in a circular or semicircular motion.

Guests share a feast which includes *Cathern cakes*, *wiggs*, and *lambs wool.* Catherine cakes are wheel-shaped cakes flavored with sugar, eggs, and caraway seeds. Wiggs are triangular or wedge-shaped biscuits with currants, glazed orange, and caraway seeds.

Lambs wool is a spicy cider. It is served from a *Cathern Bowl.* The bowl is placed on the head table under a wire wheel suspended from the ceiling. Around the wheel are twelve small apples.

Catherine argued against fifty scholars, defending her religious beliefs, and won. In memory of her victory, guests must drink from the Cathern Bowl before the festival ends, promising a year of study.

The festival ends with a display of wheel-shaped fireworks.

Cathern Wheels

Reproduce several copies of the patterns below for students to make ornaments to decorate your classroom or take-home decorations for St. Catherine's Day. Prepare a table with margarine tub lids, oatmeal boxes, milk cartons, Popsicle™ sticks, 8" (20.32 cm) construction paper circles, and paper plates. Provide students with crayons, markers, scissors, glue, a hole punch, and ribbon to assemble their decorations.

1. Color and cut out the wheels.
2. Glue one wheel to the center of a construction paper circle.
3. Punch a hole at the top of the circle.
4. Lace and tie a length of ribbon through the hole for hanging.
5. Glue the remaining patterns to margarine tub lids, an oatmeal box, or to a Popsicle™ stick to make more Cathern wheel decorations.

St. Martin's Day

St. Martin's Day is celebrated in several European countries during the month of November. In many countries the celebration is held in honor of Martin of Tours, an officer in the Hungarian army, who cut and shared half of his coat with a beggar. St. Martin is also known as a friend of the harvest. In some countries the celebration honors Martin Luther, a German priest born in the sixteenth century.

Sharing Wheel

Cut a 17" (43.18 cm) poster board circle. Divide the circle into pie slices to match the number of students in your class. If you have an odd number of students add your name to the pie. Write each child's name on one of the slices. Punch a hole at the center of the pie. Cut a 9" (22.86 cm) oaktag arrow and attach it to the center of the pie with a brass fastener, making sure the arrow moves freely.

Mount the circle to a 17" x 22" (43.18 x 55.88 cm) contrasting colored poster board. Write "Sharing Wheel" at the top of the poster board. Use the sharing wheel to match students to work or study together or to be buddies during a field trip.

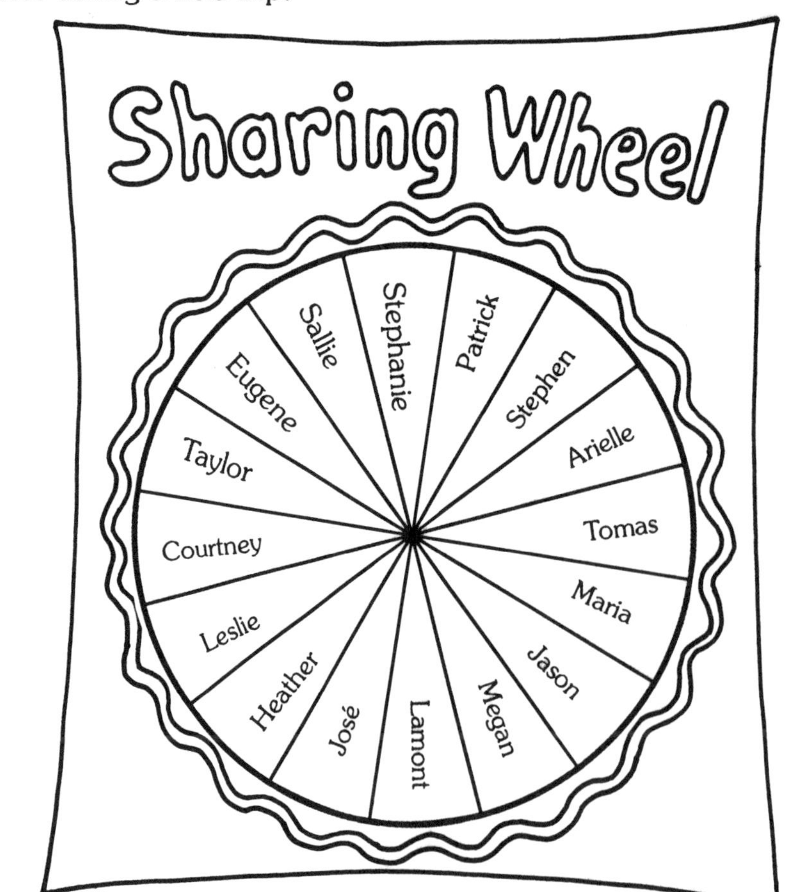

Sukkot

Sukkot, also called the Festival of Booths, is one of the three Jewish High Holidays celebrated at the end of the autumn harvest season.

This harvest festival, which falls on the fifteenth and sixteenth days of the Hebrew month of *Tishri* (September-October), is believed to have originated with an ancient holiday when religious ceremonies were held to encourage rainfall after a grape harvest. And for seven nights ancient farmers lived in booths made from fruit and evergreen tree limbs known as *succahs*, Hebrew for tent or booth.

Today, Sukkot is celebrated as a thanksgiving festival. Families build traditional *succahs* using branches and leaves, making sure the *succah* does not have anything placed over it. Modern succahs are decorated with fruit, handmade ornaments, paper garlands, and pictures. In Israel, a succah or sekhakh is made of carob tree branches like the ones used two thousand years ago. Many families eat all their meals and sleep under the stars in their succahs during the entire holiday like their ancient ancestors.

Sukkot Door Garland

Reproduce the patterns on page 156 for student-made Sukkot door decorations and garlands. Provide students with ribbon, crayons, markers, scissors, and glue to complete this project. Make additional garlands to drape around windows, bulletin boards, chalkboards, and desks.

Sukkot Door Garland

1. Color and cut out the patterns.
2. Punch a hole at each dot.
3. Lace a length of ribbon through the holes as shown.
4. Continue adding patterns to make a garland.
5. Drape the garland around a door, window, or desk.

Thanksgiving Day

Thanksgiving festivals are celebrated all over the world. The origins of these celebrations are varied but the meaning is the same—to give thanks.

Many ancient cultures held thanksgiving festivals at the close of the harvest season. One ancient harvest festival was held by the Druids of Britain, later known as *Harvest Home*. Food from the harvest was given to the poor and sometimes letters accompanied baskets of food.

Some countries celebrate Thanksgiving during the spring months because of their position in relation to the equator. Countries north of the equator celebrate Thanksgiving during the months of October and November, and those south of the equator celebrate the holiday during the month of May.

Canadians celebrate Thanksgiving on the second Monday of October, and the United States celebrates it on the fourth Thursday of November. Thanksgiving festivals are also celebrated in the Virgin Islands during November; however, there are times when they celebrate Thanksgiving during October after a season of fair weather.

Harvest Mobile

Decorate your classroom with student-made harvest mobiles. Provide students with construction paper fruit and vegetable shapes, a paper plate, scissors, a hole punch, yarn, crayons, and markers.

Have students decorate and punch holes around the edge of a paper plate and through harvest patterns. Show how to lace and tie a length of yarn to each pattern, then to the paper plate. When the mobiles are completed, punch two holes in the center of the paper plates. Lace and tie a length of yarn through the holes for hanging.

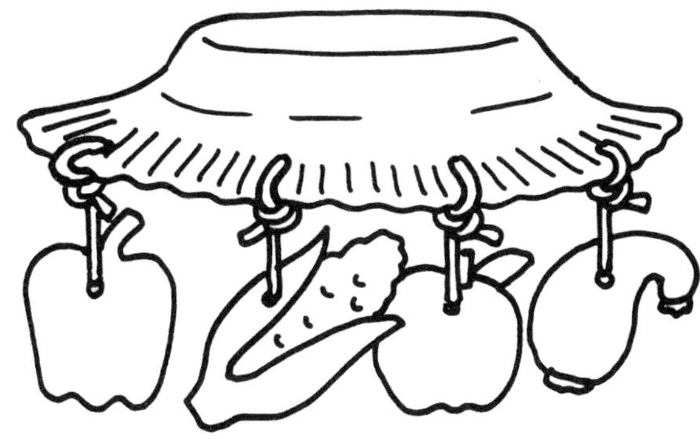

Yom Kippur

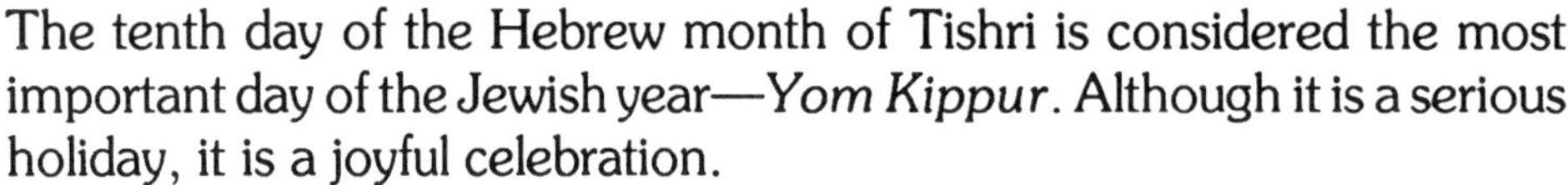

The tenth day of the Hebrew month of Tishri is considered the most important day of the Jewish year—*Yom Kippur*. Although it is a serious holiday, it is a joyful celebration.

During this holiday, everyone over thirteen years of age fasts (taking no food or drink) during the entire twenty-four-hour day and no business is conducted. Traditionally the entire day is spent in synagogues where religious services are conducted which include the reading of the biblical story of Jonah and the Whale.

Families gather for a large meal on the eve of Yom Kippur, before the twenty-four-hour fast begins (at sunset). Candles are lit and family members ask to be forgiven for their wrongdoings. White, considered a symbol of purity, is the traditional color used during this holiday in synagogues. It is also used for the caps worn by the congregation.

Jonah and the Whale Collage

Reproduce the patterns on page 159 for students to make Yom Kippur collages. Provide students with blue and green construction paper to make cutout waves, crayons, markers, scissors, sand, glue, a 12" x 18" (30.48 x 45.72 cm) sheet of construction paper, and a variety of craft supplies.

1. Color and cut out the patterns.
2. Assemble and glue the patterns to a sheet of construction paper.
3. Add details to your picture with crayons, markers, and other craft supplies.
4. Write your name at the top of your collage.

Jonah and Whale

International Flag Festival

Pages 162-186 feature flags from nations all over the world that celebrate national holidays and independence days during the autumn months of September, October, and November.

Reproduce the flags for students to color and cut out. Provide a blank sheet of construction paper for students to draw and color flags for countries you would like to include that are not featured.

Provide each student with crayons, markers, scissors, glue, and a sheet of colored construction paper on which to mount his or her flag. Add one extra inch (2.54 cm) to the length of the paper as a fold-over margin. Have students glue finished flags on the sheets as shown below.

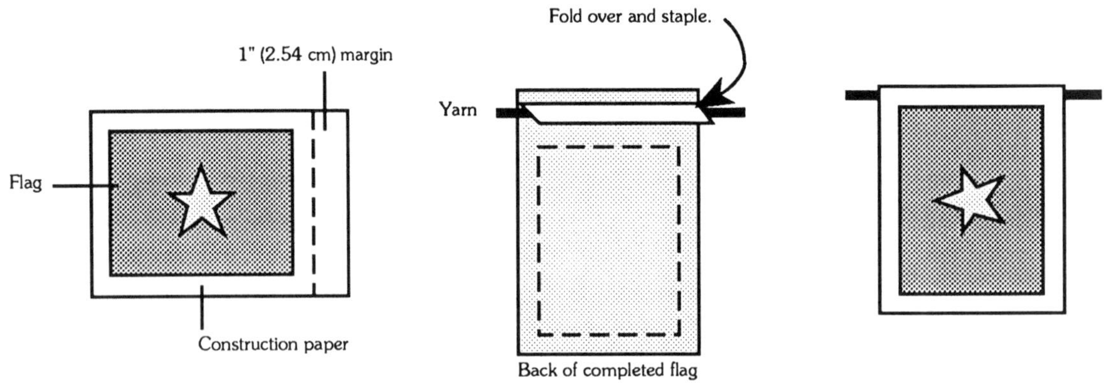

Drape colorful lengths of yarn or ribbon streamers around your classroom. Show students how to attach their flags by folding the 1" (2.54 cm) margin over the string and securing with staples.

Enlarge the flags of countries listed on page 161 for students to color and display in the center of the bulletin board. When the season is over, let children take their projects home to share with their families.

To dress up student work, follow the directions listed on page 21 in the Antarctica section. Provide students with crayons, markers, scissors, glue, poster board, plastic straws, and cellophane tape.

International Flag Festival

The countries listed below celebrate national holidays and independence days during the autumn months of September, October, and November.

Mideastern and African Countries
Peoples Republic of Angola
Peoples Republic of Benin
Republic of Guinea
Republic of Lebanon
Kingdom of Lesotho
Democratic Republic of Madagascar
Republic of Mali
Islamic Republic of Mauritania
Federal Republic of Nigeria
Sultanate of Oman
Kingdom of Swaziland
Republic of Turkey
Republic of Uganda
Yemen Arab Republic
Republic of Zambia
Republic of Zimbabwe
Central and South American Countries
Republic of Brazil
Republic of Chile
Republic of Costa Rica
Republic of El Salvador
Republic of Guatemala
Republic of Honduras
United Mexican States
Republic of Nicaragua
Republic of Panama
European Countries
People's Socialist Republic of Albania
Federal Republic of Austria
People's Republic of Bulgaria
Federal Republic of Germany
Malta
Principality of Monaco
Most Serene Republic of San Marino
Russia, formerly Union of Soviet Socialist Republics
Socialist Federal Republic of Yugoslavia

International Flag Festival

International Flag Festival

International Flag Festival

ORNAMENTS & DECORATIONS

International Flag Festival

International Flag Festival

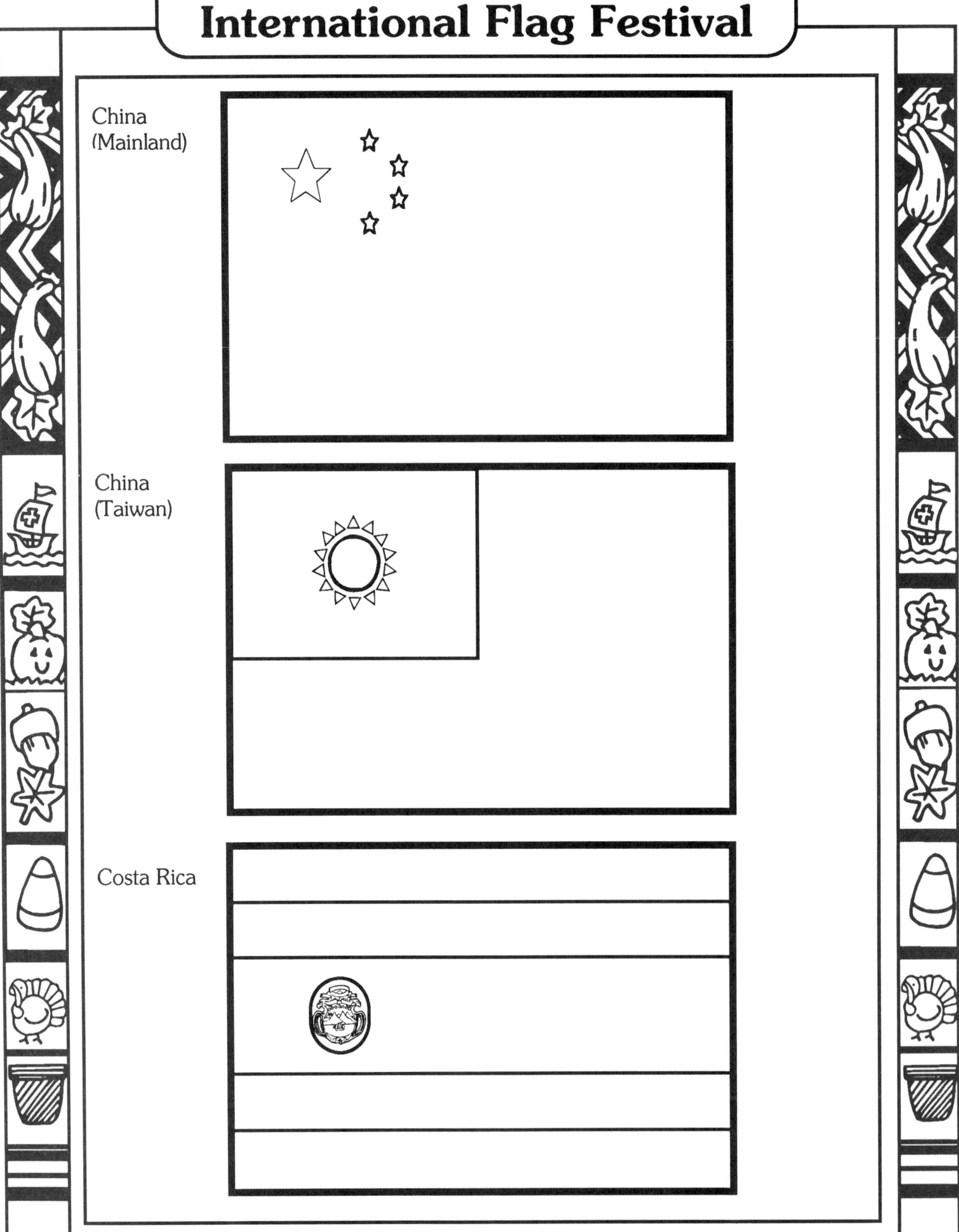

International Flag Festival

International Flag Festival

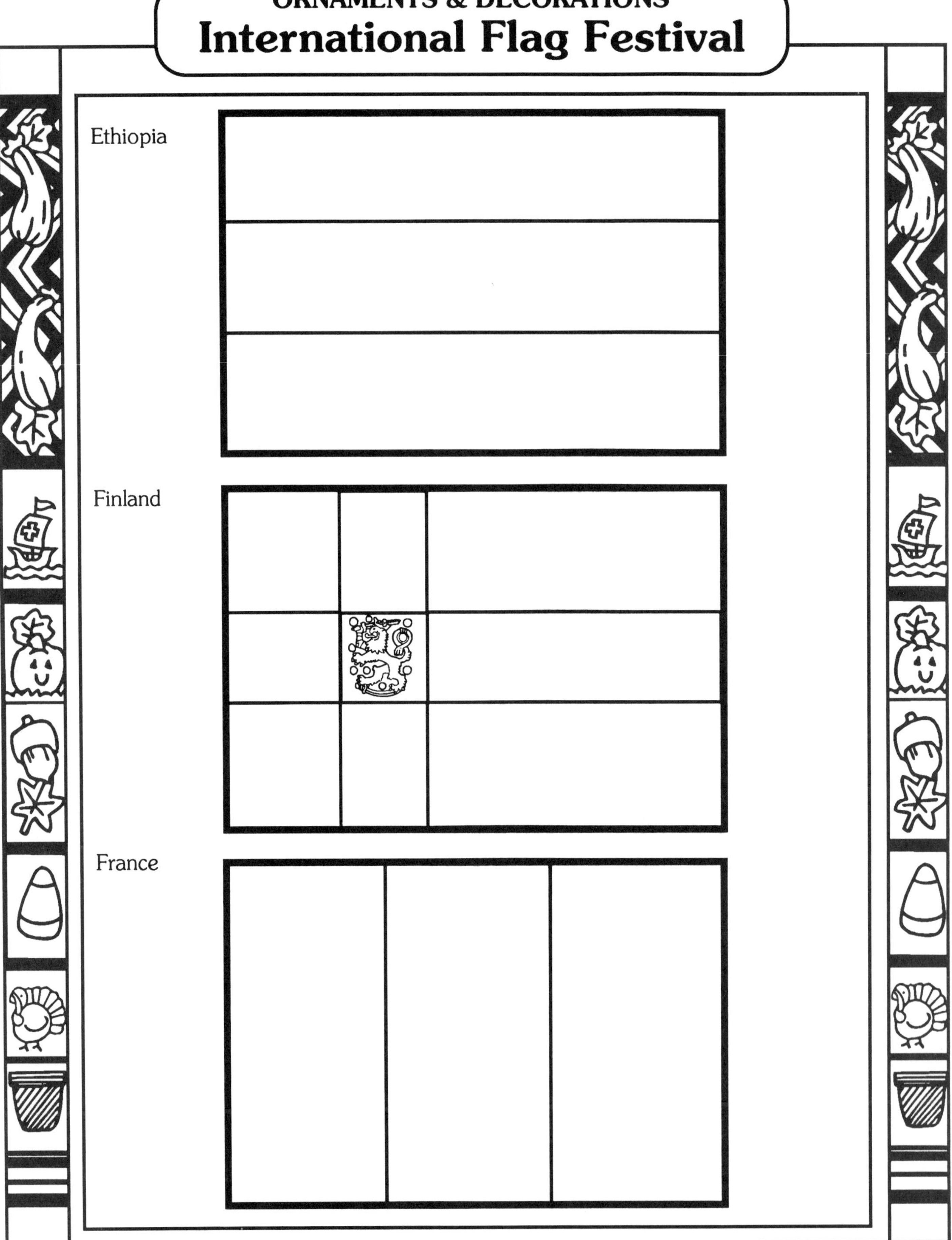

International Flag Festival

International Flag Festival

International Flag Festival

International Flag Festival

International Flag Festival

International Flag Festival

International Flag Festival

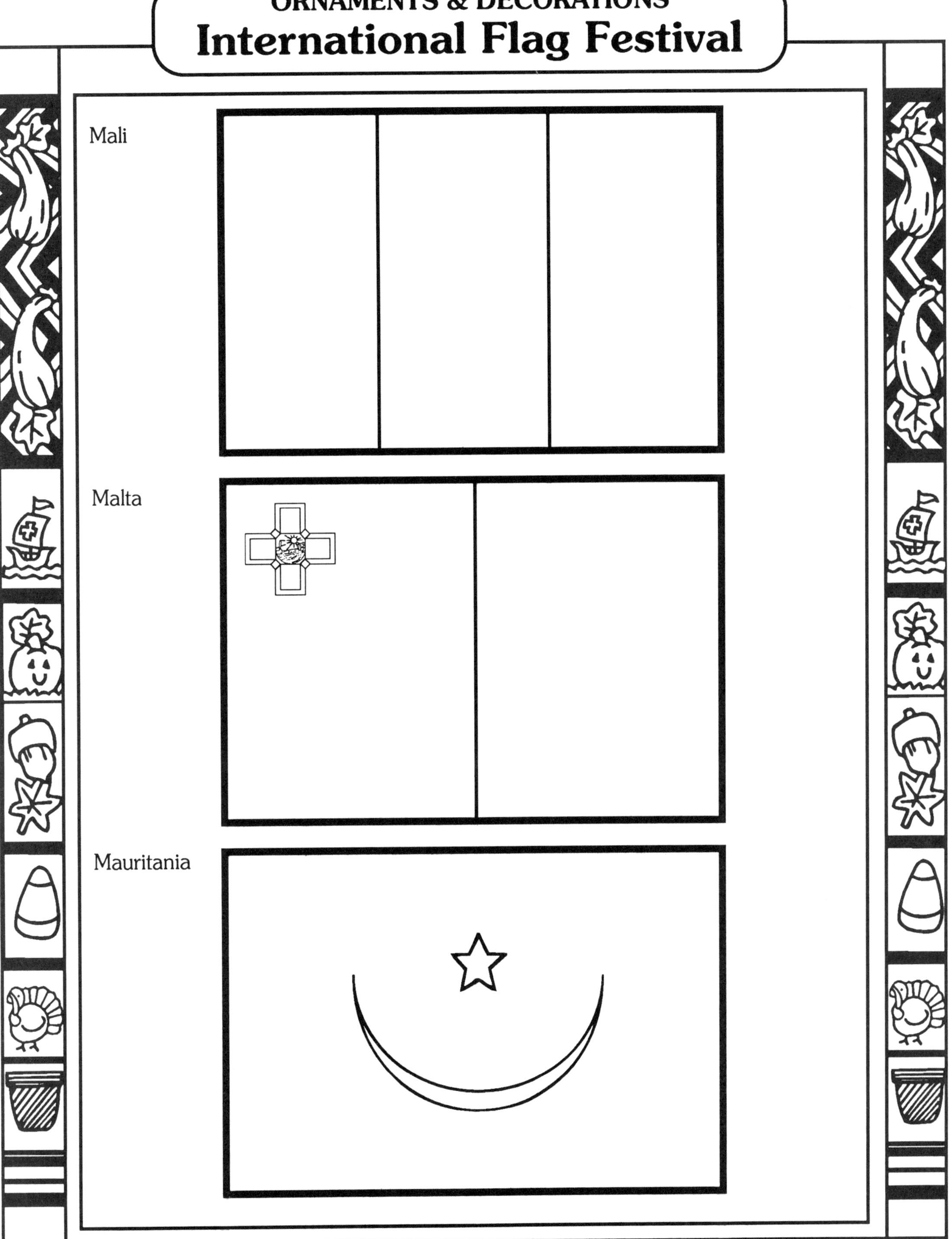

International Flag Festival

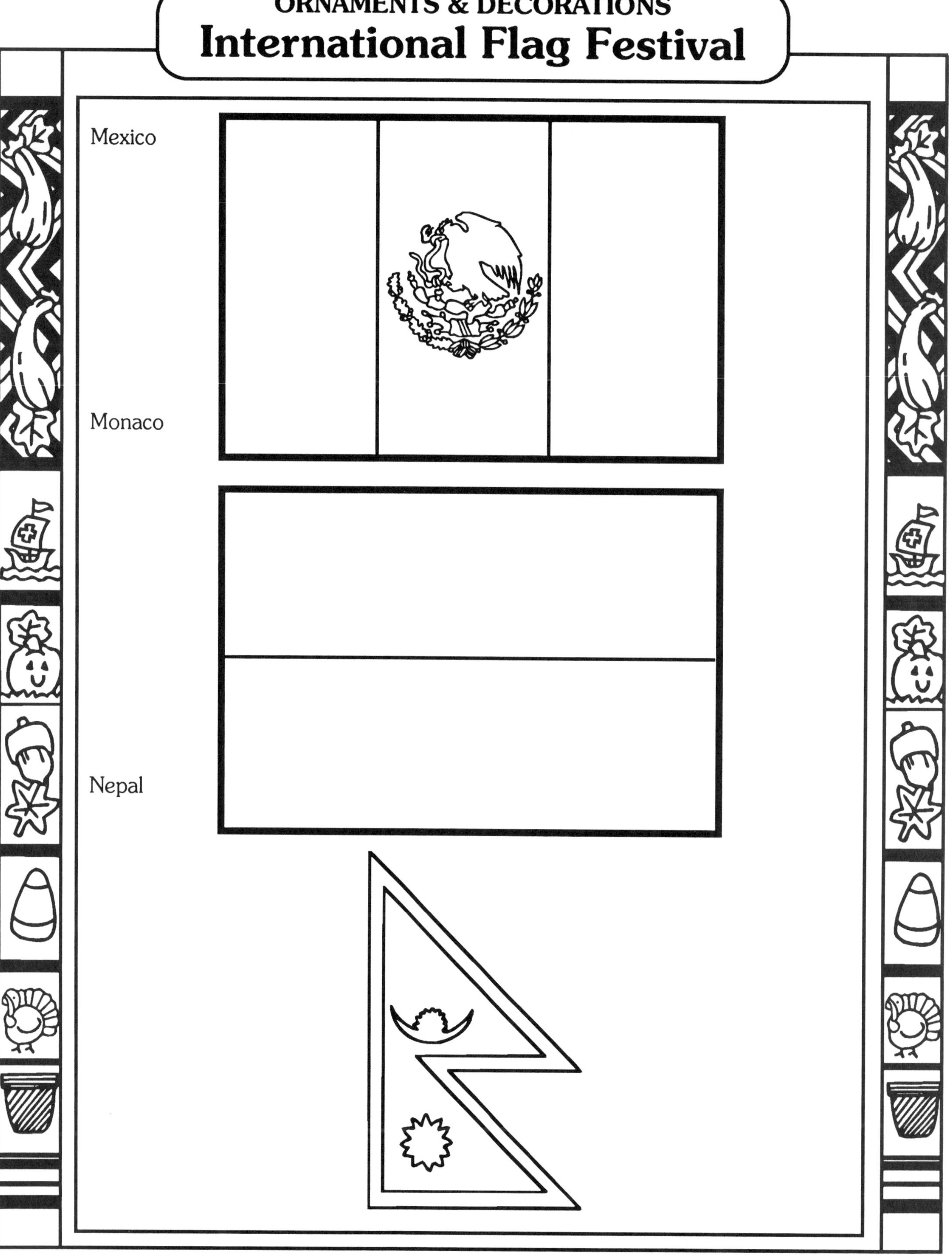

International Flag Festival

New Zealand

Nicaragua

REPUBLICA DE NICARAGUA
AMERICA CENTRAL

Norway

International Flag Festival

International Flag Festival

International Flag Festival

ORNAMENTS & DECORATIONS

International Flag Festival

ORNAMENTS & DECORATIONS

International Flag Festival

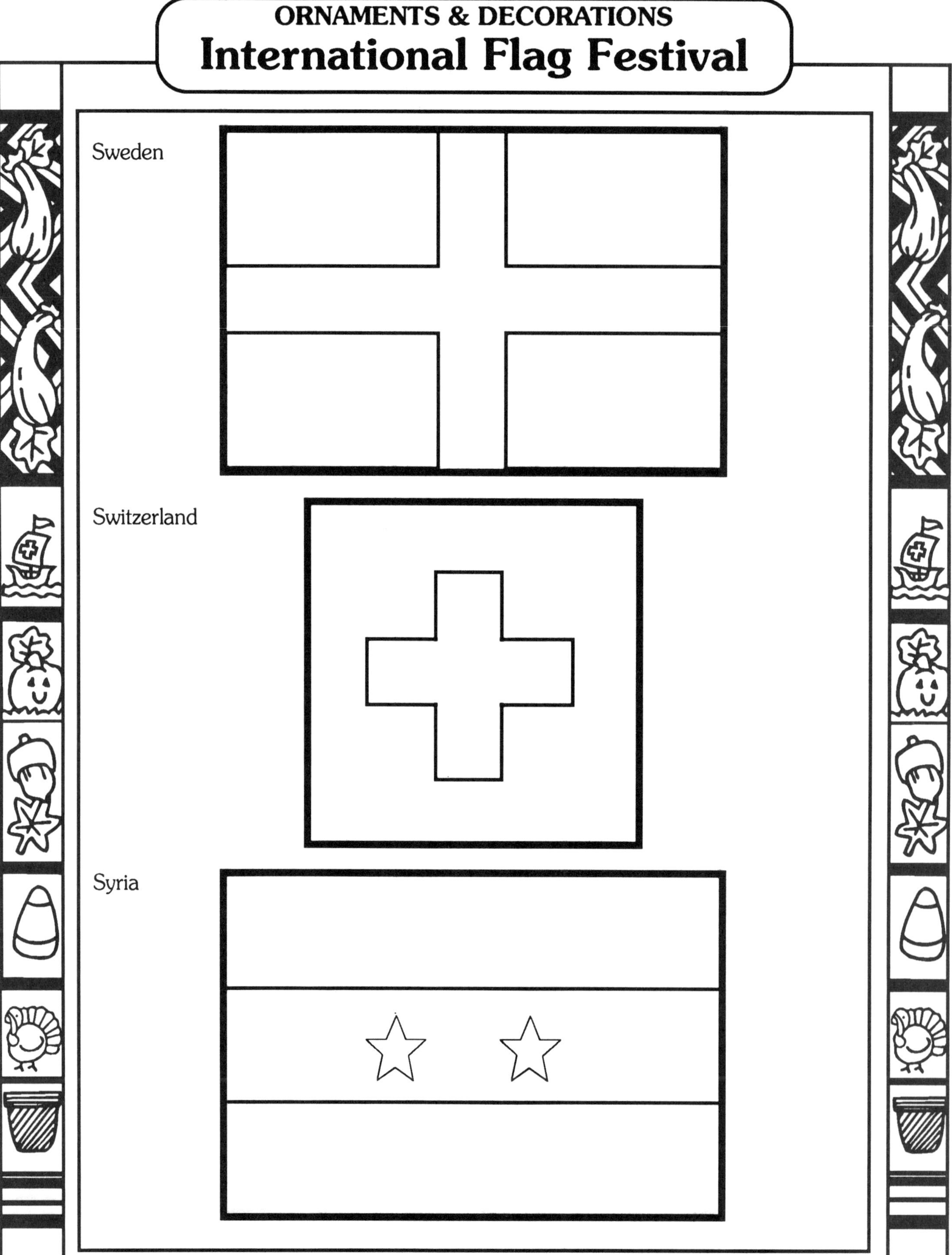

International Flag Festival

International Flag Festival

ORNAMENTS & DECORATIONS

International Flag Festival

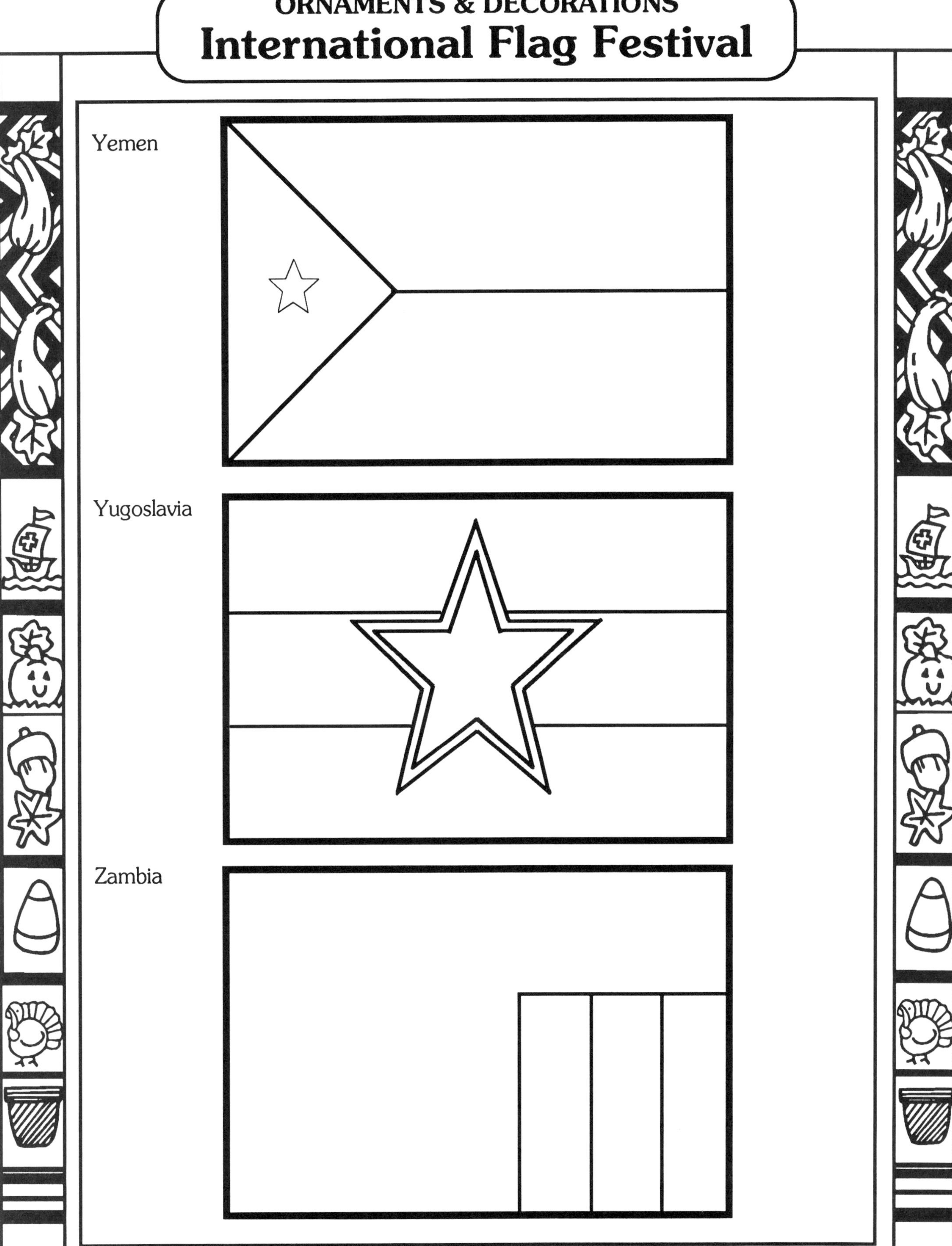

ORNAMENTS & DECORATIONS

International Flag Festival

A TAKE-HOME NOTE FROM

AROUND THE WORLD

____

Date

Dear __________________________,

We are ______________________________________

____.

Please ______________________________________

Thank you!

____

Teacher

Bibliography

Holidays Around the World
by Carol Greene
published by Regensteiner Publishing Enterprises, Inc.

Medieval Holidays and Festivals
by Medeleine Pelner Cosman
published by Franklin Watts

Festivals
by Ruth Mannig-Sanders
published by E.P. Dutton & Co., Inc.

Festivals for You to Celebrate
by Susan Purdy
published by J. B. Lippincott Company

The Celebration Book of Great American Traditions
by Wicke Chambers and Spring Asher
published by Harper & Row, Publishers, Inc.

Holiday Parties
by Judith Streb
published by F. Watts

The Thanksgiving Book
by Willard Scott
published by Dell Publishing Co., Inc.

Projects for Autumn and Holiday Activities
by Joan Jones
published by Garrett Educational Corporation

European Folk Festivals
by Sam and Beryl Epstein
published by Garrard Publishing Group

Chase's Annual Events
published by Contemporary Books

The Volume Library
published by The South Western Company and Hammond Inc.

World Book Encyclopedia
published by Field Enterprises Educational Corp.

The Folklore of American Holidays
published by Gale Research International Limited

The Folklore of World Holidays
published by Gale Research International Limited